International Internships and Volunteer Programs

International Options for Students and Professionals

by
Will Cantrell and
Francine Modderno

by

Will Cantrell and
Francine Modderno

assisted by Marianne Janney

ISBN 0-941541-02-9
Library of Congress Cataloging-in-Publication Number 92-081534

Distributed by:

Contents

Section I.
Government and International Organizations

Internship & volunteer opportunities with government and international institutions. The list includes both U.S. government and international government organizations.

Section II.
Academic Programs

Internships tied directly to a college credit-granting program, with a program of accompanying study involved; however, you do not need to be enrolled at a particular institution to participate. Tuition for the internship is required.

Section III.
Independent Internships and Traineeships

Internship opportunities not tied to an academic program, both paid and unpaid, both in the United States and abroad.

Contents

Section IV.
International Volunteer Opportunities with Private Organizations

Mostly non-profit organizations. Most positions are unpaid, although some positions may be paid either partly or wholly by the organization, while some positions entail expenses paid by the volunteer.

Section V.
Miscellaneous Work Opportunities

Miscellaneous work opportunities that are not strictly internships or volunteer positions, but that also are of interest.

Introduction

What's to be gained from an internship or volunteer program? A lot. The label of "stepping stone" with regard to an internship may be overused, but it's still accurate. An internship is an entry-level opportunity, an invitation to learn about a new field. It's not an opportunity to make your financial fortune, but a chance to learn how to make a contribution through a professional discipline. The practical insight gained from an internship or volunteer experience, and professional contacts made, can determine how you spend the rest of your professional life.

Pertinent work experience is the most formidable obstacle to an international career. Internship and volunteer opportunities featured in this book can help you overcome that obstacle by providing work experience in the international arena, or even in a foreign setting. Indeed many of the organizations you can work for as an intern or volunteer will offer you a salaried position, once you've proved yourself. (It's their best recruiting tool!)

Many of us, especially at mid-life, feel a need to get off the merry-go-round and make a meaningful contribution—to experience the gratification we sometimes lack in our work. The daily stimulation and excitement of seeing the world through another's eyes has its own rewards and the satisfaction of knowing you've helped improve even a small part of our planet is immediately gratifying. Such an experience is likely to change your life, or at the least enhance it, for years to come.

As you'll soon discover by reading this book, there are numerous opportunities of international scope for interns and volunteers in a variety of career fields and with a variety of organizations, both public and private. The career fields include government, politics, law, journalism, business, finance, film, theater, publishing, marketing, public relations, health care, science, social work, agriculture and a host of others.

In our first section we list opportunities with national and international government organizations and institutions, such as the World Bank. These opportunities include cooperative education or work-study programs, traditional internships and volunteer opportunities, such as those offered by the United Nations. Some are semester programs, some are summer programs and a few are for up to two years in duration. One program offered by the Peace Corps allows participants to combine a year of on-campus work with a standard two-year assignment as a Peace Corps volunteer, with the objective of receiving a master's degree upon completion of service. Some of these positions are paid, some are unpaid. Most are with the U.S. offices of these organizations, but several are with overseas offices, such as the Munich office of Radio Free Europe/Radio Liberty.

Section II of this book lists internships tied directly to a college credit-granting program, with accompanying study involved. Most of these positions are overseas. Although many are sponsored by a college, such as Georgetown University or Boston University, you do not need to be enrolled at that particular institution to apply for the program. Tuition for the internship is required. For most of these programs, you need to be an undergraduate or graduate student, and a few require proficiency in the language of the country where the position is located. The duration of these internships is for a semester, summer or a year.

Section III lists internship opportunities with international or internationally-focused organizations that are not tied to an academic program. You must secure these positions directly from the organization offering them. If you want college credit, you must arrange that separately through your college or university. Most of the positions are with the American offices of these organizations. Several of the organizations offer positions overseas. One example of the latter is the International Association of Students in Economics, which offers traineeships in 69 countries. Most of these organizations are non-profit lobbying groups, such as the African-American Institute or Amnesty International. Several are associations, such as the American Bar Association, which offers internships in law firms overseas, or the American Society of Travel Agents, which offers internships each year to attend its annual World Travel Congress. Several are private companies, such as Beijing-Washington, Inc. Most of these internships are unpaid.

Section IV of this book lists volunteer opportunities with private, non-profit organizations, such as Food for the Hungry. Most of these positions are overseas and usually are for a year or longer. Some of the programs offer small stipends, most offer living accommodations and board. Some require volunteers to pay for their own transportation to and from the host country. Some require volunteers to pay a fee to cover program administration costs. Most of these positions are in relief and development work or health care. Several, such as the International Medical Corps, are strictly for health care specialists, such as physicians and nurses. One organization, the International Executive Service

Corps, is a network of retired executives who provide technical and business management expertise to other countries on a volunteer basis. Another, La Sabranenque, uses volunteers to help restore historical buildings in France and Italy. Many of the positions presented in this section are with religious organizations.

Section V lists miscellaneous opportunities that are not strictly internships or volunteer positions, but that also may be of interest to those seeking international experience. These include opportunities such as an au pair program; Earthwatch, which sponsors overseas working vacations, at the participant's expense; and the Student Exchange Employment Program, which arranges independent paid temporary work for American students.

An assignment as an international intern or volunteer can provide some of the more meaningful and active experiences of your life, as well as illuminate the path toward an international career. It's up to you to make the most of it!

Section I

Government and International Organizations

This section lists internships and volunteer opportunities with government organizations and international institutions. It includes both U.S. government and international government organizations.

The Agency for International Development (AID) is a U.S. government agency that helps people in developing countries acquire knowledge and resources to build economic, political and social institutions.

AID has several student work programs that may lead to permanent employment and perhaps eventually overseas work.

Cooperative Education Program

The Cooperative Education Program (Co-op) combines academic classroom learning with practical, on-the-job experience. In addition to providing students with a paid work experience in their field of study, the program offers the opportunity for full-time professional employment through non-competitive appointment to government service upon successful completion of the work-study program.

AID accepts applications for co-ops in accounting, business administration/management, government contracting/procurement, information resources management, computer science and economics.

College students accepted for appointments as accountants work two full-time, six-month periods, alternated with academic study. Co-op appointments in other areas may be on a more flexible schedule. High-school students typically work half-days throughout the school year. Upon satisfactory completion of the program, a student may work an additional 120 days, during which time he or she may be appointed to a competitive professional position.

Requirements

The program is open to full-time high-school, undergraduate and graduate college students in accredited institutions who are working toward a certificate, diploma or degree. Students must be at least 16 years of age, U.S. citizens, maintain at least a 2.5 grade-point average, and pass a background investigation.

To complete the program, high school, graduate and technical school students must work a minimum of 640 hours; undergraduate students, a minimum of 1040 hours.

Participating schools must have a Cooperative Education Program; students must participate in their school's program and must apply through their school's Co-op coordinator.

Volunteer Intern Program

AID offers internships to students considering careers in international relations. Positions are available in a variety of disciplines according to the needs of the various bureau offices. Opportunities are in public health, political science, international relations, business management, agriculture, private enterprise, environmental science, economics and other areas.

Requirements

Internships are available to currently enrolled students who are taking at least a half-time academic course load, and who will continue their education immediately upon completion of the internship. You must have a 2.5 grade-point average or higher. To apply, send a completed SF-171 (Application for Federal Employment), a recent transcript of grades, a letter describing your interest in an AID internship, and a letter of recommendation from a school official. All employees of AID must pass a background investigation; therefore, applications for internships should be made three months prior to the anticipated date of entry on duty.

Stay in School Program

This program offers employment to students who, because of financial constraints, may not be able to continue their education without paid employment. The program is open to high-school students and those continuing education immediately after high school.

Students are appointed at civil service grades GS-01 through GS-04 and may work a maximum of 20 hours per week when school is in session, and full time during school holidays. Jobs include messenger and clerical positions, typing and other support positions. Appointments are for one year and may be renewed upon recertification of financial need.

Requirements

You must be a U.S. citizen, at least 16 years of age, enrolled in school full time, certified according to the economic guidelines established by the U.S. Office of Personnel Management, and be able to pass a background investigation.

Summer Aide Program

The Summer Aide Program is similar to the Stay in School Program except that students are paid only at the federal minimum wage. Special skills are not required. Jobs may include messenger work, filing, mail handling, light typing, etc. The program runs from May 13 through September 30.

Requirements

Requirements are the same as for the Stay in School Program, mentioned above. Summer aides must be referred to AID for employment by local offices of the State Employment Service.

Summer Employment Program

AID offers summer employment opportunities for currently enrolled students as interns, clerks and clerks/mail clerks. Summer internships may be paid or unpaid, depending on agency policy. Students do professional work in the area of their academic studies.

Summer clerks must be able to verify their ability to type 40 words per minute. Summer clerks/mail clerks need not have typing skills, as the work includes mail sorting, distribution, etc. Summer employment begins May 13 and ends September 30.

Requirements

Applicants must be U.S. citizens, at least 16 years of age, and enrolled full time in school.

Application Procedures for All Programs

Applicants for all programs must submit an SF-171 (Application for Federal Employment); college students must include a transcript of grades or OPM form 1170/17 (List of Courses). The SF-171 and OPM form 1170/17 can be obtained from your nearest federal government office or from AID itself. A background investigation also is required.

Contact for All Programs:

Agency for International Development
Office of Human Resources Development
   and Management
2401 E Street, N.W.
Washington, D.C. 20523-0105
ATTN: Student Programs Coordinator

The Central Intelligence Agency (CIA) provides to the president of the United States information on trends and current events abroad. The CIA coordinates the nation's intelligence activities by collecting, evaluating and disseminating intelligence that directly affects our national security. The agency correlates the efforts of several federal intelligence organizations and provides U.S. government policy-makers with the information they need to formulate foreign policy.

The CIA offers several internship and student programs. It also offers tuition assistance to those who plan to return to the agency for full-time employment.

Graduate Studies Program

The CIA's Graduate Studies Program offers summer internships for students entering or continuing graduate school. The program focuses on languages, international affairs, area studies, economics, engineering, geography, cartography, political and strategic research, psychology, medicine, law or other sciences.

For the student, a CIA internship provides an opportunity to participate in the substantive work of the agency. The results of graduate fellows' research projects usually are of high quality and some are published. For the agency, the program provides an opportunity to assess the analytical ability and potential of graduate fellows for permanent employment. About 25 percent of the fellows become permanent CIA employees after completion of their studies.

Requirements

You must be accepted for admission to graduate school during the fall following the summer of internship. Those whose initial applications look promising will be sent a formal application and invited to Washington at agency expense for interviews, tests and a medical examination. You must undergo a polygraph test and a complete background investigation. Deadlines are October 15 for initial application query and January 15 for sending the official application.

Student Trainee Program

The CIA's Student Trainee Program is a cooperative education program for promising undergraduate students. It offers the student an opportunity to gain practical work experience in combination with his or her academic field of study. The program is for students of engineering, computer science, mathematics, physics, political science and economics.

The student trainee is paid for the internship, according to the percentage of his or her course work that is completed, and salaries are competitive with those paid in the private sector.

Requirements

CIA student trainees are selected only from academic institutions that have established co-op work-study programs. They alternate periods of study at school with periods of work for the agency. They are expected to spend from three to six periods on the job, depending on whether the school is on a quarter or semester system. Students are interviewed from four to six months in advance of their availability. Considerable importance is placed on the student's interests, suitability and academic performance. Student applicants must undergo the same medical screening, background investigation and polygraph interview given applicants for regular CIA full-time positions. There is no specific deadline for applying, but applicants must apply six months in advance of the first semester or quarter they are considering. Interviews must be conducted four to six months before their availability. Students must be U.S. citizens and must be able to work a minimum of three work terms, on an alternating basis, prior to graduation. They must have a minimum 2.75 grade-point average and their school must have an established co-op work-study program.

Undergraduate Scholar Program

The Undergraduate Scholar Program offers graduating high-school students, particularly minorities, a unique opportunity to work in challenging positions with the CIA during the college summer. Student Scholars also receive tuition assistance and a salary throughout their college career. When they complete the program they are expected to continue employment with the agency after graduation for a period of one-and-a-half times their college career.

Requirements

You must have a minimum high-school or college grade-point average of 2.75 on a four-point scale. If in college, you must be a full-time student enrolled in a four- or five-year college program. Deadline for application is no later than the end of your first semester of senior year in high school or the first semester as a freshman in college.

Minority Undergraduate Studies Program

In the Minority Undergraduate Studies Program, promising minority undergraduates gain practical summer work experience to complement their academic studies.

Requirements

You must have a minimum grade-point average of 2.75 on a four-point scale, and you must have completed one or two years of college-level academic study. Application deadline is mid-September.

Career Trainee Internship Program

Under the Career Trainee Internship Program, students interested in a career in overseas intelligence operations participate in a nine-week course designed to introduce them to the CIA and its programs. Many have the opportunity to return to a permanent position in overseas work with the CIA. Students participate in the internship program during the summer between their junior and senior year in college or first and second year in graduate school. If they qualify for a staff position after completing the internship and are willing to commit to at least 18 months of agency service after graduation, they will be offered full tuition assistance for their final year of study.

Requirements

You must have a minimum grade-point average of 3.0 on a four-point scale. You must be a full-time student enrolled in your junior year of college or first year of graduate school.

Application Procedures for All Programs

Send a letter of application, including your name, address, phone number, major, year in school and grade-point average.

Contact for All Programs:

Student Programs Office
P.O. Box 1255
Department IEH
Pittsburgh, PA 15230

International Finance Corporation

The International Finance Cooperation accepts interns for summer employment in its Washington headquarters.

Requirements

Applicants must be available between June and September. Each applicant must be registered as a full-time, degree-seeking student who will be returning to school at the end of the summer period to continue his or her studies. Students selected from abroad must have received permission to work from the Immigration and Naturalization Service, or their sponsors, prior to commencing employment.

You must have at least a bachelor's degree or equivalent academic training. Students just completing their university degrees in the spring term will be considered only if they submit written verification that they have been accepted for, and intend to pursue, additional studies.

You must have a solid academic background, with studies primarily in finance, business administration, accounting, statistics, computer science, and/or economics, and you must have some relevant experience. All summer positions require a good working knowledge of computer software. A few positions require French or Spanish skills.

Application Procedures

Applications must be received by the end of February, and will not be accepted after that time. Send a resume and cover letter indicating interest in the Summer Employment Program to the corporation.

Contact:

Summer Employment Program
International Finance Corporation
1818 H Street, N.W., Room I-2001
Washington, D.C. 20433

INTERNATIONAL MONETARY FUND

The International Monetary Fund (IMF) began its operations in 1946. It was conceived to promote international monetary cooperation and to help produce a free system of world trade. The Fund concerns itself with the economic problems of its 156 member countries and formulates policies to stabilize the world financial situation. The largest group of specialists are economists.

Interns work at IMF headquarters in Washington, D.C., for ten to 13 weeks during the summer. Work is usually on a research project under the supervision of a senior member of the staff. The program is designed to attract qualified young economists, who may be considered for permanent positions after completing their graduate work. Interns receive a stipend of about $2,200 per month, economy round-trip airfare to Washington, D.C., and optional medical insurance.

Requirements

Applicants must be nationals of IMF member countries, with good academic records and successful completion of most of their graduate work in economics. Academic emphasis should include monetary economics, public finance, international economics and econometrics. Effective oral and written communication in English is a must.

Application Procedures

IMF's application for employment or a curriculum vitae with all university-level economics courses should be sent before January 31. Candidates will be interviewed if possible, or required to submit two essays. Interns will be notified in mid-March.

Contact:

Summer Internship Program
International Monetary Fund
Recruitment Division
Room 6 - 525
700 19th Street, N.W.
Washington, D.C. 20431

The Organization of American States (OAS) is the oldest regional organization of nations in the world. It was established in 1890, at the first American Conference of American States. Some of the organization's purposes are to promote peace and security in the hemisphere, solve economic and political problems among its members, and encourage cooperative action. The General Secretariat in Washington, D.C., is the central headquarters for OAS operations.

The General Secretariat sponsors unpaid internships for college students preparing for careers in public service. Students work with the professional staff of OAS and do a variety of jobs, including research, writing, designing projects and administration. The organization tries to match the students' interests and skills when assigning a department. Internships can be for a semester or for the summer. During the semester programs, interns work at least 16 hours per week. Summer interns are expected to work full time. Interns must participate in an orientation program that teaches them about the work and goals of OAS. This program is carried out through weekly seminars with various staff members. Interns are required to present a monthly and final written evaluation of their experience. It may be possible for students to qualify for college credit by serving in one of these internships.

Requirements

Applicants should be nationals of member nations and be in the last two years of their undergraduate work or in a graduate program. They should have at least a 3.0 grade-point average. Applicants should be fluent in Spanish, since about 80 percent of OAS's work is conducted in that language. OAS prefers applicants who have a working knowledge of Portuguese and/or French, as well as English and Spanish.

Application Procedures

The official OAS application form must be submitted with two letters of recommendation and a transcript. It is preferred that one recommendation be from a professor in your major field of study and the other from a former employer. Applications for the fall session are due June 15; for the winter/spring session, November 15; and for the summer session, March 15. It is requested that telephone calls regarding the internship program be placed between 10:00 a.m. and 12:00 p.m. or between 3:00 p.m. and 4:00 p.m.

Contact:

> Organization of American States
> Mrs. Mary Baldwin, OAS Internship Coordinator
> 1889 F St., NW, Seventh Floor
> Washington, D.C. 20006
> telephone (202)458-3519

The Overseas Private Investment Corporation (OPIC) is a self-sustaining, U.S. government agency whose purpose is to promote economic growth in developing countries by encouraging U.S. private investment in those nations. By so doing, OPIC can help American companies remain competitive in the international marketplace. OPIC was established by Congress in 1969, and began operations in 1971. It assists U.S. investors through two principal programs: (1) financing investment projects through direct loans and/or loan guarantees, and (2) insuring investment projects against a broad range of political risks.

OPIC uses interns in such departments as finance, insurance, corporate communications, development and general counsel. Interns may work full time or part time during the fall, winter, or summer semesters. The internships are unpaid, but academic credit can be arranged.

Requirements

U.S. citizenship is required and applicants must be enrolled in a relevant academic program at the time of the internship. Undergraduates or graduate students may apply, but graduate students in finance, international studies or international affairs are given first consideration. Applicants should have good written and oral skills, a foreign language, and have completed some computer course work.

Application Procedures

Send two copies of the following: a resume, a cover letter, a short analytical writing sample, list of relevant courses and OPIC reply form.

Contact:

Overseas Private Investment Corporation
Brenda Hardy
Intern Program Coordinator
1615 M Street, NW
Washington, D.C. 20527
telephone (202)457-7094

The Peace Corps is a U.S. government-funded volunteer organization whose purpose is to promote world peace and friendship through one-on-one technical assistance to other countries.

Not only does the Peace Corps have a regular and associate volunteer program, but its Office of University Programs also offers several programs in collaboration with colleges and universities for individuals interested in joining the Peace Corps. They include the Peace Corps Preparatory Program, the Masters Internationalist Program, the Community College Model and Campus Compact internships.

Peace Corps Volunteers

Peace Corps volunteers work on a wide variety of projects in developing countries, ranging from digging ditches to setting up small businesses. Most work in agriculture, forestry, vocational training, health programs, English teaching and construction projects. The Peace Corps has two volunteer programs: the regular volunteer program and the associate volunteer program. (See the next section for information on the associate volunteer program.)

Regular volunteers are recruited for two-year assignments. As language proficiency is essential, all regular volunteers receive three months' intensive language training in their host country. They also

---

receive training in cultural studies to familiarize them with the history, customs and political system of the country in which they will work. Regular volunteers are limited to serving only one tour with the corps. Volunteers with almost any background can be chosen, but of special interest are those with experience or degrees in the life sciences (biology, botany, physics, chemistry) and with environment-related skills and training.

Regular volunteers receive free housing, travel expenses, health benefits and a monthly living allowance, plus a "salary" that amounts to about $200 per month. The salary is retained by the agency for payment upon completion of service, and is considered a "nest egg" to enable the volunteer to start out again in the United States upon his or her return. The "nest egg" adds up to about $5,000. Upon completion of service, regular volunteers also receive a special non-competitive preference rating for employment with other government agencies. This special preference for government jobs is effective for three years. Regular volunteers also are eligible to defer payment on their National Direct Student Loans while they are in the service.

Requirements

There are almost no restrictions on applicants other than that they be at least 18 years of age. Handicapped candidates are welcomed to apply. As mentioned above, the Peace Corps does have a preference for applicants with experience or training in agriculture, health, teaching, accounting, engineering, physical and occupational therapy, and special education or related disciplines, although anyone interested is encouraged to apply.

Associate Volunteer Program

The Peace Corps' Associate Volunteer Program is aimed to utilize the services of highly skilled, technically oriented professionals who are unable or do not wish to interrupt their career, but who can devote anywhere from three to 15 months to the program. The Peace Corps has worked out collaborative agreements with a number of American school systems, universities, corporations and unions to make it possible for employees to take leaves of absence from their work in order to participate in the Associate Volunteer Program.

Participants in the Associate Volunteer Program are considered Peace Corps volunteers, subject to the same evaluation and general placement standards as two-year volunteers. They accrue many of the same benefits. They may not, however, be eligible to receive the non-competitive preference status in competing for federal government positions that regular volunteers receive on completion of their Peace Corps service, nor may they be eligible for the privilege to defer payments on National Direct Student Loans.

Requirements

Professionals with the following skills particularly are sought for the Associate Volunteer Program: health-related skills, teacher training, veterinary science, environmental science, financial management, university teaching and vocational education. Language ability and/or prior overseas experience are an advantage.

Application Procedures for Both Volunteer Programs

A packet of application materials will be sent to you for one or both volunteer programs upon a letter or telephone call of inquiry. For both programs, contact the address below.

Contact for Both Volunteer Programs:

Peace Corps
Volunteer Recruitment
1555 Wilson Boulevard, Suite 701
Arlington, VA 22209

The Peace Corps Preparatory Program

In this program, students may design their undergraduate programs to increase their chances of being successful applicants for Peace Corps service. In many instances, the Peace Corps is able to make early commitments about placement for students who successfully complete these "Peace Corps Track" programs, and who also qualify under standard Peace Corps health and fitness criteria. Early commitment possibilities are limited to fields of study that qualify as "scarce skills" and/or those programs that can help enrich the racial and ethnic diversity of the volunteer corps.

Currently, there are Peace Corps Preparatory Programs at Grinnell College, Norwich University, the University of Florida, School for International Training, the University of the South and Johns Hopkins University.

The Master's Internationalist Program

Individuals in this program typically would combine a year of on-campus work with a standard two-year assignment as a Peace Corps volunteer in an appropriate field. Upon completion of service, the volunteer would be awarded a master's degree in his or her field of study. Some of these programs require the compilation of a diary during overseas duty, while others require the completion of a thesis or paper after close of service. These programs have a tremendous benefit for applicants whose undergraduate work is in a liberal arts program and who normally would have to wait for longer periods of time to qualify for a generalist placement opportunity in the Peace Corps. By participating in one of the Master's Internationalist Programs, they can use their waiting time to qualify for a scarce-skill placement for which the Peace Corps can pre-clear them. Fourteen schools thus far participate in this program.

The Community College Model

In this program, the Peace Corps takes graduates of two-year programs in key skill areas, marries them with specialized Peace Corps training, and connects them with four-year degree-granting institutions willing to offer academic credit for Peace Corps training and experience. The goal is to satisfy the requirements for a baccalaureate degree with perhaps two semesters of on-campus work at the conclusion of service.

Campus Compact Internships

The Peace Corps offers undergraduate internships to students who want to work for a semester or a quarter in Peace Corps offices overseas. About 250 colleges and universities participate in this program. These internships are competed for, with each Campus Compact institution able to nominate one candidate. The internships last 10 to 15 weeks and placements are made in the fall, winter, spring and summer. The countries and jobs vary with the needs of the Peace Corps. Among the jobs interns might do are compiling or analyzing data, organizing resource libraries, or giving training in computer operations or word processing.

The schools provide transportation to the work site and medevac insurance; Peace Corps provides transportation to stateside pre-service training, as well as housing for the interns in-country. Information and applications are sent to Campus Compact member schools in February. Applications are due by May 1, and notification is by June 1.

Student Internships

Students may apply for regular internships throughout the Washington office of the Peace Corps, where they may learn about the work of the agency.

Cooperative Education

The Peace Corps has a program of cooperative education with several schools willing to identify students who want a semester's work in Washington during each of their junior and senior years as full-time Peace Corps employees. This program is aimed at minority students who are considering careers in government service or international affairs.

Application Procedures for All University Programs

For information on all Peace Corps University Programs contact the Peace Corps' University Program coordinators.

Contact for All University Programs:

University Program Coordinators
Peace Corps of the United States
1990 K Street, N.W.
Washington, D.C. 20520

Radio Free Europe/-Radio Liberty (RFE/RL) is a non-profit corporation funded by congressional grants. As a professional news and information broadcaster, it reaches over 56 million people mainly in Eastern Europe and the Commonwealth of Independent States (C.I.S.).

RFE/RL sponsors summer internships for upper-level undergraduates and graduate students. The internships usually are in three areas: C.I.S. and Eastern European research; Eastern European broadcasting research; and electrical engineering. Most of the internships are in Munich, Germany. The engineering internships are in Spain, Portugal and Germany. Interns receive a small stipend, transportation and housing.

Requirements

Applicants should be upper-level undergraduates or graduate students. It is important to have a good background in the area of the internship. Most of the RFE/RL internships require proficiency in one or more foreign languages. Applicants for the CIS and East European research internship should have a background in that area and have a good knowledge of Russian or an East European language. The broadcasting internships are for students in the following areas: international media; mass communications; market research; statistics; sociology; social psychology; or East European studies. Applicants for these internships should be competent in quantitative research methods, opinion survey methods and computer applications. Knowledge of an East European language is helpful. The electrical engineering internships are for applicants with course work relevant to international radio broadcasting. Applicants for these internships should have a basic knowledge of German, Portuguese or Spanish.

Application Procedures

RFE/RL publishes a program announcement listing current intern opportunities and requirements in November. Application deadlines usually are in mid-February.

Contact:

Radio Free Europe/Radio Liberty
Intern Program
Personnel Division
1201 Connecticut Avenue. NW
Washington, D.C. 20036
telephone (202)457-6936

The United Nations offers both volunteer and internship opportunities. The programs are as follows.

The United Nations Volunteers Program

The United Nations Volunteers (UNV) program has been in operation since 1971. About 75 percent of the volunteers serve in Africa, and most of the rest in Asia or the Pacific. Only about 1.5 percent are in Latin America. In the United States, the Peace Corps acts as the sponsoring agency for U.S. citizens who wish to become U.N. volunteers.

The UNV program places U.S. volunteers with specialized or technical skills in countries where no Peace Corps programs exist. Previous volunteers have served in Turkey, the Sudan, the Maldives, Uganda and Chad. Volunteers usually are assigned to work with other volunteers from different countries. No formal orientation or any training is given to volunteers. Occasionally they are briefed in Geneva on their way to their assignment, but usually they receive a briefing only from the project manager or U.N. representative.

The Peace Corps provides round-trip transportation to the assigned country. It also will pay transportation expenses for up to two dependent children. UNV pays a living allowance that is about the equivalent of $450 per month. Housing, in-country transportation, health insurance and life insurance also are provided by UNV. The Peace Corps pays U.S. volunteers a readjustment allowance upon completion of their assignment. The rate is approximately $200 per month of service.

The placement process for volunteers usually takes a minimum of six months. Once assigned, volunteers are expected to leave within six weeks of acceptance by the host country.

Requirements

Applicants must be at least 21 years of age. A degree or technical diploma and at least two years of relevant work experience are required. Fluency in English, French or Spanish is required. Volunteers must be fluent in the language of the assigned country, so there may be additional language requirements. These languages include English, French, Spanish, Arabic or Portuguese.

Application Procedures

U.S. volunteers first must complete the Peace Corps application in order to gain sponsorship (obtain this by writing to the first Peace Corps address below). The Peace Corps application should be returned to the nearest Peace Corps office. The Peace Corps then will send you a UNV application form.

The UNV Personal History Statement (PHS) must be typed. It is important to attach copies of all pertinent documents such as diplomas, birth certificates for children, or certification of any special training. A passport-sized photo also should accompany the application. This form and all supporting documents should be sent to the second address below (the Peace Corps/UNV office).

Contact:

Peace Corps Recruiting Office
1990 K Street, NW
5th Floor
Washington, D.C. 20526
telephone (800)424-8580 ext. 226 or 238
    or (202)254-4940

Peace Corps
United Nations Volunteers
International Operations
1990 K Street, NW
Washington, D.C. 20526

United Nations Internships

Hiring of interns, like the hiring of professionals, by agencies of the United Nations is decentralized. There is no single office that coordinates all internships associated with the United Nations. The question of whether or not to maintain an internship program often is left up to individual branch offices of U.N. agencies. As such, most U.N. internship programs are shaped largely by the priorities of the office involved.

A few programs have been institutionalized by consistent administration over the years. They have the same requirements, duties and application procedures each year and relatively are unaffected by changes in office personnel.

Interns are not paid and are responsible for travel costs and living expenses.

Department of Public Information Internships

Every summer the Department of Public Information conducts the Graduate Student Intern Programme in New York and the Graduate Study Programme in Geneva. The New York program runs for a four-week period in June and July, and the Geneva program for two and a half weeks in July and August. Participants have an opportunity to expand their understanding of the United Nations' principles and operating procedures through lectures, discussions, first-hand study and work assignments with U.N. staffers. The Geneva program is conducted in English and French.

Application Procedures

Candidates should apply in writing to their own college or university. Application forms are provided to the Office of the Dean of the relevant graduate schools at each participating institution.

Contact:

(Applicants for the New York program)
Coordinator of the DPI Graduate Student Intern Programme
Room S-1037G
Department of Public Information
United Nations
New York, NY 10017

(Applicants for the Geneva program)
The United Nations Office at Geneva
Information Service
Palais des Nations
CH-122 Geneva 10
Switzerland

Ad Hoc Internship Programme

The Ad Hoc Internship Programme is a "hands-on" orientation to the workings of the United Nations. The program lasts for a minimum of two months and applications of those willing to work one or more full academic terms are welcome. A number of graduate schools give academic credit to their students for successfully completing such an internship with the United Nations. Although arrangements can be made to allow the intern to pursue part time his or her own interests in study or research related to the United Nations, an intern is expected to devote a minimum of two and a half days a week to the department to which he or she has been assigned.

Most assignments are at U.N. headquarters in New York. There are plans to expand the program to cover other duty stations, and, if appropriate, applicants should indicate any interest in an assignment outside New York.

Requirements

The program is open to graduate (and, in special cases, to exceptional undergraduate) students who believe in the principles and activities of the United Nations and who are supported strongly by their schools for internship.

Application Procedures

Graduate students should write to the internship coordinator, enclosing, where possible, a filled-out *ad hoc* internship application form from the Ad Hoc Internship Office, any permanent mission to the United Nations, or the office of the dean of the relevant graduate school of their university. Transcripts of grades or lists of courses taken, and a sample of research work, if available, should be included.

Contact:

Internship Coordinator
Recruitment Programmes Section
Room 2500
Office of Personnel Services
United Nations
New York, NY 10017

UN Institute for Training and Research Internships

The United Nations Development Programme (UNITAR) accepts a small number of visiting scholars and interns for work in research, training or administration, for periods varying between two months and one year.

Application Procedures

Applications should be sent through the appropriate permanent mission to the United Nations or directly from the sponsoring university or institute.

Contact:

> Executive Director of UNITAR
> 801 United Nations Plaza
> New York, NY 10017

United Nations Development Programme
Summer Internship Program

The United Nations Development Programme (UNDP) has a summer internship program lasting eight to 10 weeks during the summer, which provides on-the-job training for students involved in graduate studies. It enables participants to obtain first-hand practical experience in the operations of the world's largest program of multilateral technical assistance in developing countries. Interns are expected to contribute effectively to the activities of the field office, or, in the case of a headquarters assignment, the division or bureau to which they are assigned. Every attempt is made to take into consideration the particular interests and specializations of interns when assigning them.

Interns are expected to observe normal office working hours and to undertake their assignments for the full duration of this period. They participate in a three-day induction course on UNDP policies and procedures at the beginning of their assignments.

Requirements

Students must satisfy UNDP's minimum educational and language requirements, which are: they must be studying at the post-graduate level in development-related studies and have proficiency in two of UNDP's main working languages (English, French and Spanish). Applicants also must have demonstrated a keen interest in the field of development.

Application Procedures

Send a letter of interest and a resume.

Contact:

Chief, Recruitment Section
(Summer Internship Programme)
Division of Personnel
UNDP
One United Nations Plaza
New York, NY 10017

U.N. Fund for Population Activities Internships

Internships with the U.N. Fund for Population Studies (UNFPA) provide on-the-job training for a limited number of bright young students undertaking development-oriented graduate studies, and enable participants to obtain first-hand practical experience in the operations of the world's largest multilateral assistance for the formulation and implementation of population policies in developing countries. Every attempt is made to take into consideration the particular interests and specialization of an intern when assigning him or her to a specific area or responsibilities.

Internships generally take place during the summer months. The intern is expected to observe normal office working hours and to undertake his or her assignment for the full duration of this period.

Requirements

Students must satisfy UNFPA's minimum educational and language requirements: they should be pursuing a graduate degree in development-related studies, and be proficient in two of the United Nations' working languages (English, French and Spanish). They also are expected to have demonstrated a keen interest in the field of development.

Application Procedures

Application consists of a completed U.N. Personal History Form, a passport-sized photograph, and a brief statement of motivation, outlining your interests and reasons for wishing to participate in this type of program. A letter of endorsement from a senior faculty member who has directly supervised you in the recent past, and who is fully acquainted with your background, is appreciated.

Contact:

> Chief, Recruitment Section (Internships)
> United Nations Fund for Population Activities
> One United Nations Plaza
> New York, NY 10017

International Labor Office Internships

The International Labor Office (ILO) is a specialized agency of the United Nations with 150 member countries. It seeks to improve working conditions, create employment and promote human rights around the world.

ILO offers internship opportunities in the following areas: recruitment, personnel, marketing, publications, technical information and public affairs. Each program is approximately 15 to 20 hours a week. Internships vary in duration according to the program. Location of internships is usually in the branch office in Washington, D.C. Programs are offered on the basis of the intern's needs.

There is no salary, but the cost of local transportation to and from the office will be reimbursed.

Requirements

Studies in relevant topics are required of the applicant.

Application Procedures

Send a letter of interest and a resume.

Contact:

> International Labor Office
> Personnel Office (Internships)
> 1828 L Street, N.W., Suite 801
> Washington, D.C. 20036

International Atomic Energy Agency Internships

Since 1957, the International Atomic Energy Agency (IAEA) has served as the world's central intergovernmental forum for scientific and technical cooperation in the field of the peaceful use of nuclear energy. IAEA's fundamental mission is to assist countries in their peaceful uses of the atom in agriculture, health, energy, and other fields; and to apply its safeguards on nuclear materials and facilities so as to verify that they are not used for military purposes. At present, there are 113 countries in IAEA's membership.

The purpose of IAEA's internships is to provide the intern with the opportunity to perform work in line with his or her own career or to perform a task in line with his or her studies and interests, which will, at the same time, be of benefit to the agency's programs. Internships are unpaid. Duration of an internship normally is not less than one month and not more than a year.

Requirements

The applicant must be working or studying in a relevant discipline.

Application Procedures

Send your curriculum vitae and indicate the length of time and the dates you wish to work.

Contact:

International Atomic Energy Agency
Personnel Office (Internships)
Wagramerstrasse 5, P.O. Box 100
A-1400 Vienna
Austria

Addresses of Other UN Organizations

The Internship Coordinator
UNICEF
Three United Nations Plaza
New York, NY 10017

World Health Organization
1211 Geneva 27
Switzerland

United Nations High Commission for Refugees
Case postale 2500
CH-1211 Geneva 2 Depot
Switzerland

Food and Agriculture Organization
of the United Nations
Liaison Office for North America
1001 22nd Street, N.W., Suite 300
Washington, D.C. 20437

International Bank for Reconstruction
    and Development
1818 H Street, N.W.
Washington, D.C. 20433
International Monetary Fund
19th and H Street, N.W.
Washington, D.C. 20431

General Agreement on Tariffs and Trade
Villa le Bocage
1211 Geneva 10
Switzerland

United Nations Conference on Trade and Development
Palais des Nations
1211 Geneva 27
Switzerland

United Nations Development Program
366 United Nations Plaza
New York, NY 10017

United Nations Educational, Scientific
    and Cultural Organization
UNESCO House
Place des Nations
1211 Geneva 20
Switzerland

Universal Postal Union
Weltpoststrasse 4
Bern, Switzerland

World Meteorological Organization
41 Avenue Giuseppe Motta
Geneva 20
Switzerland

The United States Army Judge Advocate General's Corps (JAGC) hires 100 law students (75 second-year and 25 first-year) each summer to work as legal interns in Army legal offices throughout the United States and overseas.

Interns work under the supervision of an attorney and perform legal research, write briefs and opinions, conduct investigations, interview witnesses, and otherwise assist in preparing civil or criminal cases. Duties performed by a military attorney in a typical Army law office include: providing legal advice and assistance to soldiers and their families on personal legal matters (e.g., domestic relations, wills, consumer problems, land-lord/tenant issues, tax questions, and immigration and naturalization matters); reviewing government contracts; investigating and adjudicating claims for and against the United States based on tort liability; preparing and trying criminal cases under the Uniform Code of Military Justice or in U.S. Magistrate's Court; and reviewing administrative actions for legal sufficiency under federal statutes and regulations, to include environmental issues and labor law matters.

Interns are hired as temporary civil service employees for a maximum period of 90 working days starting in May or June of each year. Students who have completed two years of law school are paid at the GS-07 federal pay level. Students who have completed one year of law school are paid at the GS-05 federal pay level. Interns must pay all costs of travel to their job location. Also, they must arrange for housing and pay all housing expenses. All interns have sponsors at the offices where they work. These sponsors can assist interns in locating housing and making other arrangements. These are not military positions and no military obligation is incurred by participating in the program.

Requirements

The Judge Advocate General's Corps Summer Intern Program seeks law students with proven scholastic ability and demonstrated leadership potential. Candidates must be full-time students at law schools accredited by the American Bar Association (ABA). Students in four-year programs are eligible for the Summer Intern Program after completion of their second year of law school. Candidates must be U.S. citizens.

Application Procedures

The application must include the DAJA-PT Form 13 (you can obtain this from the address below), a head-and-shoulders photograph, resume, and undergraduate and law school transcripts. First-year students should include any grades they have received prior to the application deadline. You also must arrange for a personal interview with a JAGC field screening officer prior to the application deadline. JAGC field screening officers interview at most ABA-accredited law schools once each fall and spring semester.

Contact:

Army JAGC Professional Recruiting Office
   (Summer Intern)
Building 1834, Franklin Road
Fort Belvoir, VA 22060-5818
telephone 1-800-336-3315
   or in Virginia, (703)355-3323 collect

The U.S. Department of State carries out U.S. foreign policy and maintains more than 230 embassies and consulates in over 140 countries. Opportunities exist for student interns in the Work-Study Program, the Paid Summer Intern Program, and the Presidential Management Intern Program. Also, State's Office of the Legal Adviser offers a Work-Study Program and a Summer Intern Program for law students.

UNITED STATES DEPARTMENT OF STATE

Student Intern Programs

Work-Study Program

More than 20 different bureaus or offices within the Department of State offer work-study internships. Most of the positions are in Washington, D.C., but there are some opportunities to serve abroad at foreign service posts. The Bureau of European and Canadian Affairs, the

Bureau of Inter-American Affairs and the Bureau of International Organization Affairs offer some of the overseas internships. Interns serve for a semester, a quarter or a summer. The work might involve research, the preparation of reports, correspondence, computer science, analysis of international issues or work in international or domestic law. Interns in the Work-Study Program receive no pay and usually work about 40 hours per week. Interns going abroad are responsible for all their own travel and living expenses. Academic credit for the internships is available from most colleges and universities.

Requirements

Applicants should have an interest in foreign affairs and be enrolled in an academic program as an undergraduate junior, senior or graduate student. The Department of State requires that all interns be U.S. citizens, have a relevant academic background for the work, and be able to pass a background investigation. Preference is given to students with a "B" average or better. Women and minority students are encouraged to apply.

Paid Summer Internships

Paid Summer Internships have been sponsored by the following bureaus or offices within the Department of State: the Bureau of African Affairs, the Bureau of Consular Affairs, the Information Systems Office, the Office of the Comptroller, the Office of the Legal Adviser, and the Bureau of Personnel. The internships begin in May and end in September each year. Interns receive temporary appointments as federal employees and their positions and pay are determined by their qualifications and educational levels. While most of the summer positions are in Washington, D.C., some of the internships are overseas.

Presidential Management Internships

These internships exist to attract highly qualified people to work in the federal government. The Department of State is one of many government agencies that is part of this program. Colleges and universities nominate graduating students to be part of this program. The selection process is very competitive, with the Office of Personnel Management choosing 250 finalists.

Presidential Management Interns receive two-year civil service appointments and the appointments can be extended for one additional year. After completing this program, interns are eligible to convert to permanent civil service status. Interns are eligible for life and health insurance benefits as well as sick and annual leave.

Requirements

Applicants for this program must be U.S. citizens and have demonstrated outstanding academic ability. It is very important that applicants have a commitment to a career in management at the federal level.

Application Procedures for All Above Programs

Applicants for the Work-Study or Paid Summer programs must submit the following: a Standard Form 171 (Application for Federal Employment); a 500-to-750-word autobiography; a certified transcript; two letters of recommendation from faculty members; and an Office of Personnel Management Form 1386 (Background Survey Questionnaire). Standard Form 171 usually is available at government offices or post offices. Form 1386 is available from the Department of State Intern Coordinator.

Applicants for the Presidential Management Intern Program should consult their faculty adviser.

Contact for All Above Programs:

Intern Coordinator
Department of State, PER/CSP
P.O. Box 18657
Washington, D.C. 20036

Office of the Legal Adviser Internships

State Department's Office of the Legal Adviser has two internship programs. This office assists in counseling the department on all legal problems arising in the course of the department's domestic and international work. Members of the office also represent or assist in representing the United States in meetings of international organizations, such as the United Nations General Assembly, and international conferences, such as Law of the Sea conferences.

The two internship programs for law students are the Summer Intern Program, which takes six students per year, and a Work-Study (Externship) Program.

Requirements

To be considered for the Summer Intern Program you must have completed your second year of law school with high academic standing. For the Work-Study Program, your internship must be tied to academic credit, which you should receive from your sponsoring institution.

Application Procedures

For the Summer Intern Program, you should include a comprehensive resume and transcripts, and submit your application no later than November 1 for the following summer.

For the Work-Study Program, you must submit a comprehensive resume and two letters of recommendation from faculty members or officials of your sponsoring institution. One of these letters must include a statement affirming that you will receive academic credit upon satisfactory completion of the proposed semester. Your application must be received at least five months before the semester for which you are applying.

Contact:

Recruitment Coordinator
Office of the Legal Adviser
Department of State (L/EX)
Washington, D.C. 20520

Voice of America (VOA) is part of the United States Information Agency. Its News and English Broadcasts Directorate (NEB) employs approximately 250 people who write, produce and broadcast news, special events, music, Americana, feature and cultural programming of interest to listeners in all areas of the world. NEB is comprised of the News Division, Current Affairs Division and Worldwide English Division, which provide daily broadcasts in over 40 languages aimed around the world.

VOA Broadcast Interns

VOA hires four interns twice a year to work in its radio broadcast newsroom. They participate in all phases of the production process, including writing, editing, producing and announcing.

Requirements

VOA's broadcast internships are for graduate students. Candidates must have a Bachelor or Arts or Bachelor of Science degree in Broadcast Journalism. They also should have a broad knowledge of current and international affairs and U.S. institutions.

Application Procedures

Applications are accepted only from January 1 through January 15 and from April 15 through April 20 each year. Send a letter of interest and resume.

Contact:

VOA Internship Program
Voice of America
Room 3521, HHS-N
330 Independence Avenue, S.W.
Washington, D.C. 20547

VOA Volunteer Intern Program

VOA has opportunities for students to serve in its Volunteer Intern Program. The purpose of the program is to aid in career decisions after graduation. Positions are unpaid.

Requirements

College students who are currently enrolled full time or half time are eligible to serve as interns.

Application Procedures

You must submit an SF-171 (Application for Federal Employment). This form can be obtained from VOA or any U.S. government office. Include a short paragraph on each of the following topics: your long-term career goals, relevant work experience, how you could contribute to the Voice of America.

Contact:

> Voice of America
> Volunteer Intern Program
> Room 1543
> 330 Independence Avenue, S.W.
> Washington, D.C. 20547

VOA English Intern Program

The English Intern Program is a two-year paid internship that can lead to a career position in international broadcasting with VOA. The purpose of the intern program is to develop further the skills of the best qualified candidates for future writing, editorial and managerial positions in VOA. Interns are trained to work in all phases of NEB feature and documentary writing, news writing and programming, voicing, production, reporting, etc. The VOA English Intern Program is highly selective and extremely competitive. Typically, finalists represent only about two percent of total applications. After successful completion of one year in the program, depending on the candidate's eligibility and the availability of positions at the time, each intern may compete for a permanent career appointment. English intern positions are filled at the civil service GS-07 level.

Requirements

The program is not for the novice, nor for one without academic background in, or practical exposure to, the broadcast communications field. Recruitment efforts are directed toward graduates of colleges and universities that have nationally known departments of broadcast journalism and communications. Without such background, one has little chance of selection.

Application Procedures

Send an SF-171 (Standard Application for Federal Employment). You can pick up the application from any U.S. government office. Application deadline is the end of April for September appointment.

Contact:

> Voice of America
> Merit Promotion, VOA/PO
> Room 1543, HHS-N Building
> 330 Independence Avenue, S.W.
> Washington, D.C. 20547

The World Bank

The World Bank offers internships at its Washington, D.C., headquarters. Opportunities are available in economics, finance, accounting and statistics. Interns are hired through the Summer Employment Program and are paid a monthly salary. These summer positions are available between June and September.

Requirements

Applicants must have an undergraduate degree and be working full time on an advanced degree for the academic year following the internship. Degrees should be in areas with business applications. Computer skills and relevant work experience are very important. Interns with the World Bank should know at least one language other than English.

Application Procedures

Send a resume before the February 28 deadline. A World Bank application and a form for summer employment will be sent. Participants are notified in May by telephone.

Contact:

The World Bank
Summer Employment Program
Room O-5079
1818 H St., NW
Washington, D.C. 20433
telephone (202)477-1234

Section II

Academic
Programs

This section lists internships tied directly to a college credit-granting program, with accompanying study involved. You do not need to be enrolled at a particular institution to participate. Tuition for the internship is required.

The American Association of Overseas Studies (AAOS) organizes internship, travel and study programs in England, France, Germany, Italy, Spain, Switzerland and Israel. AAOS charges a fee for its programs and places students according to their backgrounds with organizations in the fields of law, journalism, business, finance, film, theater, publishing, government, politics, marketing, public relations, biology and museum curatorship.

Interns work full time, Monday-Thursday, and live in a dormitory in a central part of the city. AAOS provides special orientation programs, weekend tours to historic sites and receptions where students can meet and talk with professionals in their fields of interest. Programs vary in duration, but usually last about six weeks during the summer.

Requirements

There are no definitive age requirements for AAOS programs. Applicants tend to be over 15 years of age. High-school students are accepted. The main concern is that participants have a mature and responsible demeanor and a desire for a productive work and intercultural experience.

Participants pay for all program costs, which can include tuition, lectures, workshops, shared bath, common rooms, gym and kitchen facilities, meal allowance, receptions, day trips, and overnight tours. Program costs range from $1,500 to $4,700, excluding airfare.

Application Procedures

Send a letter of inquiry to AAOS. You will receive detailed program information and application forms. Completed applications should be received at AAOS by April, although late-comers may be accepted depending upon space availability.

Contact:

American Association of Overseas Studies
Summer Internship Coordinator
158 West 81st Street, Suite 112
New York, NY 10024
telephone (800)338-2748

 **American Institute For Foreign Study**

The American Institute for Foreign Study (AIFS) is an organization that sponsors foreign study and travel programs for students. AIFS and its affiliate, Richmond College in London, sponsor a wide variety of internships in London.

Internships are available in the areas of business/economics, fine arts, lens media and design, communication, politics and social sciences. They are available during spring and fall semesters. Internships in business/economics and communications also are available during the summer. The program begins with six weeks of full-time study and then an internship period of eight to nine weeks (six weeks in the summer). Interns work full time for five days a week during the internship period. These are unpaid positions, but credit is given for the internship and other courses taken. Up to 16 hours of credit may be earned during a semester (12 in summer).

Interns are housed and have meals at Richmond College. All facilities, sports programs and social activities are open to participants in the internship program. The cost for the semester program is about $7,850. This includes tuition, room, board and a one-way flight from any of 11 departure cities. Students also must pay a student activity fee of $140 and a visiting student fee of $250. The summer program is about $4,250 for tuition, room, board and one-way transportation from any of 11 departure cities.

Requirements

This program is open to American college students with at least a 2.5 grade-point average. Students also should have worked either paid or unpaid during the two years prior to their application.

Application Procedures

Complete the application for the International Internship Program that is available from AIFS. Submit the application, a reference from a former employer and an essay about your intended internship field and experience to date. Applications for the spring semester are due mid-October, summer applications are due mid-March, and fall applications are due mid-May.

Contact:

American Institute for Foreign Study
102 Greenwich Avenue
Greenwich, CT 06830
telephone 1(800)727-AIFS, ext. 6097, 6086 or 6087, or
(203)869-9090

Beaver College has a Center for Education Abroad that has sponsored more than 15,000 American students in British universities over the past 25 years.

The school's London internship program is administered in cooperation with the City of London Polytechnic.

Beaver College Center for Education Abroad

Interns work for a term with British professionals in their field of interest. An academic project that relates to the work assignment is required, along with two courses at the City of London Polytechnic. The fee for this program is about $7,600.

New in 1992-1993 are opportunities for semester-long parliamentary internships in Dublin, in affiliation with the Irish Institute for Public Administration. The internship can be combined with a semester at the Queen's University in Belfast for qualified and highly motivated students who want to study politics and government in Ireland's south and north.

Requirements

Applicants must have completed at least four semesters of undergraduate work at a U.S. or Canadian college or university. Most of the programs require a minimum of a 3.0 grade-point average on a

4.0 scale. The London internship program requires a 3.3 grade-point average.

Application Procedures

Applications and a comprehensive catalog describing the full range of programs offered are available from the Beaver College Center for Education Abroad. The application form should be returned with a $35 application fee, 10 passport-sized photos and an official college transcript. The internship requires several additional forms that can be obtained from Beaver College. If accepted, a $500 deposit is due within 15 days of your notification. Applications for the fall and full-year programs generally are due by April 20, but some are due in March. The due date for spring applications is October 5.

Contact:

Beaver College
Center for Education Abroad
Glenside, PA 19038
telephone (800)767-0029
fax (215)572-2174

Boston University offers internship programs in London, Madrid, Moscow, Paris, Sydney and Washington, D.C. These programs combine upper-level course work with an unpaid internship, so that students can earn academic credit and gain invaluable work experience in an international environment. Each program has four components: two core courses, one elective course, and one internship course, with each component worth four undergraduate credits.

London Internship Programme

Participants in the London program may choose internships in eight different areas: the arts; advertising/marketing/public relations;

comparative law; European politics; management/finance/economics; journalism/broadcasting/film; politics and international relations; and psychology and social policy. Upon arriving in London, students receive a two-day orientation. They then attend intensive classes for four and one-half weeks. The course work is designed to provide a good background for the internship period, which lasts about eight weeks, with students working four days a week and taking one course. The London program is offered for the fall, spring and summer semesters.

The program cost is about $7,400 and includes tuition, fees, the guidance and support of the London staff, and housing in apartments rented by Boston University. Meals, books, personal expenses and transportation are additional costs for participants.

Requirements

Applicants should have a "B" average or better in their college course work and be suited to a demanding schedule where they will have to work independently.

Application Procedures

Applications should be received well in advance of the semester for which you are applying. The spring semester begins in early January, the summer semester begins in mid-May, and the fall semester begins in early September.

Paris Internship Program

The Paris Internship Program combines intensive language immersion with a nine-week internship. Internships are available in many areas, including the arts, fashion and cosmetics, advertising, government, publishing, finance, industry and tourism. Students spend the first six weeks of the program in language training, supplementing classroom language sessions with a city laboratory that forces practical, advanced use of the language. They then work full time and take an elective class for the remainder of the program. Students who can prove their fluency in French may enroll in a half-semester (eight credit) program that has a one-week orientation and an eight-week internship. The program is available for the fall and spring semesters.

Interns may choose to live with a French family or live in student housing. The full-semester program costs about $7,400, and the nine-week option costs $4,675. The program fee includes lodging, two meals per day, tuition, fees and support services.

Requirements

To be eligible for the full-semester option, students must have successfully completed four or more semesters of college-level French, with a "B" grade or better. The half-semester, eight-credit program is available only to those students who already have attained substantial oral and written fluency in French. All applicants are interviewed to determine their mastery of French.

Application Procedures

Applications are due two months before the beginning of the semester for which you are applying. The spring semester begins in January, and the fall semester begins in early September. The nine-week program begins in mid-February or mid-October.

Washington Internship Program

The Washington Internship Program offers supervised internships both on and off Capitol Hill. All students are personally interviewed by the program directors, who arrange internship placements for students in congressional offices, government executive branch agencies and organizations, public interest groups, trade associations and other institutions in and around Washington, D.C. The program is designed to appeal to upper-level students majoring in virtually any academic area. Course work focuses on various political and public policy issues, and internships are full-time, five days per week, for the entire length of the program.

Students may apply for the sixteen-credit fall or spring semester programs, or for the eight-credit summer program. Fees are $7,400 for the semester programs, and $3,775 for the summer program. The fees include tuition and lodging.

Requirements

Applicants should be juniors or seniors and must have at least a "B" average in their college course work. Good written and oral communication skills are very important. This program is particularly well-suited for those students looking for careers in law, public administration, science and technology, education, or health and human services.

Application Procedures

The application deadline for the spring semester program is in early November, for the summer and fall semester programs, mid-April.

Sydney Internship Program

The Sydney Internship Program provides students with an opportunity to study and work in a pivotal city in the Pacific Rim region. Participants choose courses from one of three program tracks: management/finance/economics; journalism/broadcasting/film; and politics and international relations. The first five weeks of the program are spent taking two core courses and acclimating to the local environment. The eight-week internship period provides a learning environment that goes well beyond classroom instruction. Previous internship placements have been in banking, journalism, broadcasting, import/export trade, finance, law and marketing. During the internship period, students work full time, four days a week, and take one course.

The program cost is $7,400 and includes tuition, fees and housing in apartments rented by Boston University. Meals, books, personal expenses and transportation are additional costs for participants.

Requirements

Applicants should have a "B" average or better in their college course work, and be suited to a demanding schedule that requires them to work independently.

Application Procedures

Applications should be received well in advance of the semester for which you are applying. The spring semester begins in early January, the summer semester begins in mid-May, and the fall semester begins in early September.

Madrid Internship Program

The Madrid Internship Program offers an intensive study-abroad opportunity that combines an internship, related course work taught by local Spanish faculty, and a homestay. The program is geared to upper-division students with a strong foundation in Spanish, and offers internships in major corporations, institutes and non-profit foundations. Students take three courses in addition to working in an internship three days per week for the entire semester. An eight-credit, eight-week summer option also is available.

The program cost for the 16-credit fall and spring semester programs is $11,455 and includes tuition, housing, board and round-trip airfare. The program cost for the eight-week summer program is $3,100 and includes tuition and housing. Students are placed in Spanish households in order to integrate them directly into Spanish society and culture through the use of Spanish language in the context of daily living.

Requirements

Internships are available to students who have completed at least five college semesters of Spanish (or the equivalent) with a "B" average or better. All applicants are interviewed to determine their mastery of Spanish.

Application Procedures

Applications are due two months before the beginning of the semester for which you are applying. The spring semester program begins in January, the summer program begins in mid-May, and the fall semester program begins in early September.

Moscow Internship Program

Scheduled to be offered beginning with the spring 1993 semester, the Moscow Internship Program will allow students to be integrated fully into Russian society through intensive language and liberal arts courses and work experience. Two program options will be available: an extended semester (20-credit) program or a regular semester (16-credit) program, depending upon the student's prior course work and language ability. The extended semester program begins with an intensive four-week language/orientation program scheduled to be held in St. Petersburg. Upon completion of the language component, students move to Moscow, where they continue with their course work to prepare for their internship. Students will intern for eight weeks, working in Moscow full time, Monday through Friday. Internship opportunities are available in multinational and joint-venture corporations, politics, literary journals, print and television bureaus, advertising and publishing, non-profit organizations, and specialized areas such as accounting.

The extended semester program will cost approximately $9,000, and the regular semester program will cost about $7,400. Program fees will include tuition, housing and partial board. Students will live in dormitories in St. Petersburg, and in Russian households in Moscow. Both the extended and regular semester programs are offered during fall and spring. During the summer, only the regular semester program will be available.

Requirements

Applicants should have a "B" average or better in their college course work. Students who have completed three to six semesters of college-level Russian or the equivalent are eligible to apply to the extended semester (20-credit) program. The regular semester (16-credit) program is available only to those students who already have obtained substantial oral and written fluency in Russian. To be eligible for the regular semester option, students must have successfully completed six or more semesters of college-level Russian or the equivalent.

Application Procedures

Applications are due two months before the beginning of the semester for which you are applying. The spring semester begins in January, the summer semester begins in mid-May, and the fall semester program begins in early September. All applicants will be interviewed to determine their mastery of Russian.

To apply to any of the above programs, write Boston University for an application.

Contact for All Programs:

Boston University
International Programs
232 Bay State Road
Boston, MA 02215
telephone (617)353-9888

CUA THE CATHOLIC UNIVERSITY OF AMERICA WASHINGTON D.C.

Catholic University offers several internship opportunities both abroad and in Washington, D.C. The School of Arts and Sciences sponsors internships in the Irish Parliament in Dublin, and the Department of Politics sponsors internships in England, Belgium and Washington, D.C.

Program in Irish Society and Politics

This program is in cooperation with Ireland's Institute of Public Administration and major Irish political parties. Interns serve as aides in Dublin to members of the Irish Parliament for a semester. Interns usually are involved in research, constituency relations, party liaison and the preparation of briefing materials. They work for 25 hours per week and usually take two or three courses.

Room and board is usually with Irish families, where the students are paying guests. The cost for room and board is approximately the same as students would pay in the United States (about $2,500) and must be paid at registration. Tuition for this semester is the same as normal tuition at Catholic University, about $5,425. Interns must pay for their own round-trip transportation to Dublin.

Requirements

This program is open to upper-level undergraduate and graduate students. Admission is based on academic achievement, presence, maturity and character. Those selected are asked to read extensively about Irish society and politics before they begin their internship.

Washington Semester

Interns work in Washington for 12 to 15 hours per week for a semester. The assignments have included working for members of Congress, congressional committees, national political parties, the American Enterprise Institute, Washington city government, and radio or television stations. Students also take specialized courses in American government and politics. Room, board and tuition at Catholic University are about $8,000 per semester.

Requirements

Students should have completed one year of college and have higher than a "B" average.

Parliamentary Internship Program - London

This internship makes it possible for students to work full time as research assistants for members of the English Parliament. The program lasts for 10 weeks from mid-May to July. Six semester-hours are awarded for the internship. Tuition for the program is approximately $1,500. Lodging and food cost another $1,500.

Requirements

This program is open to upper-level undergraduate and graduate students. Prospective interns are asked to read extensively about the British government and British politics before they begin their internship.

Program in British Politics and Society - London

This program is offered in cooperation with Leeds University. Students intern with a sponsoring legislator in Parliament and are enrolled in three related courses for the spring semester. Interns are involved in such activities as research, constituency relations, representation and party liaison. The first week of each session is spent in briefings and becoming familiar with British life. For the remainder of the semester, interns work full time for their sponsor. Grades are based on a log of activities, written work for sponsors, assigned essays, weekly seminars and written assignments due three weeks after returning to the United States. Tuition for the semester is approximately $5,425, and room and board is about $2,500.

Requirements

Applicants should be upper-level undergraduate or graduate students. Academic achievement and maturity are important selection factors.

Application Procedures for All Programs

Submit the application for the specific internship program along with a transcript and references. Catholic University requires an oral interview and a test of written expression for applicants to these programs.

Contact for All Programs:

The Catholic University of America
Parliamentary Internship Program
Dr. John A. Kromkowski, Director
Department of Politics
Washington, D.C. 20064
telephone (202)635-5000

The College Consortium for International Studies (CCIS) was founded in 1975 to provide low-cost and high-quality international programs for students at member colleges and universities. The consortium has more than 150 member schools and offers programs in 17 countries. Internships are offered at the CCIS program in London, England.

The London program has semester internships available in business/public relations, criminal justice or legal studies, politics/government, social work, education and psychology. The internships are combined with academic study at Ealing College. Students usually carry 12 to 15 credit hours, including the internship. All students are required to take a course titled "Colloquium on British Culture."

Students can choose from several housing options while they are in London. They can live in British homes with breakfast and dinner provided, have bed and breakfast in a private residence, or rent rooms and do some of their own cooking. The cost of the program per semester is about $3,895. This includes tuition, room and board (two meals per day), CCIS fees, an International Student ID Card, all travel that is part of the academic program, and textbook rental. Students are responsible for round-trip transportation, some meals and personal expenses.

Requirements

The program is for undergraduates who are sophomores or above. Freshmen may apply if they have an outstanding academic record. Applicants should have a 2.5 cumulative grade-point average or above. Students should have completed related course work in the area in which they are seeking an internship.

Application Procedures

Students living in New York State or attending a four-year SUNY institution should apply directly to Rockland Community College to receive credit. Rockland's Center for International Studies sponsors the London program. For other students, Rockland will coordinate registration at a nearby institution with a CCIS program. Applications and other materials should be sent to Rockland.

Submit the CCIS application with a $30 application fee, an official college transcript and three references. Two of the references must be from college professors. Freshman should have their high-school records sent.

Contact:

Rockland Community College
Center for International Studies
Jody Dudderar, Coordinator
145 College Road
Suffern, NY 10901
telephone (914)356-4650

or

CCIS
301 Oxford Valley Road
Suite 203 - B
Yardley, PA 19067
telephone (215)493-4224

Educational Programmes Abroad (EPA) is a non-profit educational organization that recruits students in American universities for internships abroad. The EPA organizes and administers programs in Europe and Australia.

Internships in Europe

EPA arranges unpaid internships in London, Paris, Madrid, Bonn and Brussels. Those lasting a semester or longer also involve academic courses. All commence with an orientation, and in non-English-speaking countries include intensive language orientation as well. Internships that cover a semester are for at least three days per week and earn half the semester credit if taken in conjunction with two academic courses.

Internships that cover the shorter summer and quarter programs are for a full five-day work week.

In London, internships are in advertising, business studies, education, health care, law firms, medical research, museums and art galleries, politics and pressure groups, retailing, social sciences, theater or town planning. In Paris, Bonn, Brussels and Madrid, internships are in politics, business, social science or museums.

Housing is either with families, in apartments or hostels. A substantial part of the program fee is refunded on a monthly basis to help students cover board and lodging expenses. Program fees vary from $3,500 to $7,800.

Requirements

Applicants must be juniors, seniors or graduates by the time the program begins, with a grade-point average of 3.0 or above. Applications for the fall semester must be in by May 1st; for the spring semester, by mid-November; for the spring quarter, by March 1st; for summer programs, by mid-April. Your own school may have deadlines of its own.

Academic Political Internships in Melbourne, Australia

In this program, organized by the University of Melbourne, students intern with State of Victoria government officials or with members of state political parties. In addition, they take two academic courses. The program lasts for 16 weeks, from mid-February to early June.

All students receive a monthly refund, which covers board and lodging in either a family home, a hostel, Melbourne Student Village or an apartment. Lodging is secured by the student after arrival in Melbourne. The basic program cost of about $6,600 includes placement, tuition, administrative and instructional costs, orientation, room and board monthly refund, and medical/hospital student insurance. Transportation to and from Melbourne is paid by the student.

Requirements

Students must have either junior or senior standing, and a grade-point average of 3.0. You should have previously completed a course that provided some understanding of Australia's political process. Application deadline is November 15.

Application Procedures for Both Programs

You must discuss the program with your school adviser and get approval from the relevant department of your home university or college to enroll in the program. You then must fill out an EPA application form, attach your transcripts and a passport-size photo, and submit these materials to the Study Abroad Office on your home campus. Your home university will decide if you are to be accepted into the program. If you are accepted they will send your documents on to the relevant Program Center.

Contact for Both Programs:

> Educational Programmes Abroad
> 2815 Sarles Drive
> Yorktown Heights, NY 10598
> telephone (914)245-6882
> fax (914)245-6811

THE FORD FOUNDATION

The Ford Foundation is a non-profit organization that works to reduce hunger and poverty in the Third World. The foundation sponsors summer internships in the United States and abroad.

Interns have been involved with developing country programs, urban poverty programs, an international affairs program and with organization administration. They usually assist the program officer by reviewing funding requests, evaluating grants and preparing program documents. Some internships offer research opportunities. Previous interns have served in Mexico, Brazil, Egypt, Kenya, Bangladesh, India, the Philippines and Indonesia. Interns in the United States work at the New York City headquarters of the Ford Foundation. Those in New York are paid approximately $2,000 to $2,400, and overseas interns receive about $1,000, plus housing.

Requirements

Applicants must be current graduate students who will be returning to school for the fall semester after the internship. Many of the internships require a background in the social sciences. Applicants should have good analytical and writing skills. Overseas assignments require a knowledge of the country of assignment and language proficiency.

Application Procedures

Internships usually are announced in the fall for positions starting the following summer. Information and application procedures are available from placement and career-planning offices at colleges and universities. Completed application materials usually are due by early December.

Contact:

The Ford Foundation
Joan Carroll, Manager Employment & Training
320 East 43rd Street
New York, NY 10017
telephone (212)573-4794

Friends World College of Long Island University combines academic study with overseas experience, field study and internships. All of its students do internships and field studies in eight regions of the world. It has a main campus on Long Island and seven program centers around the world. These centers are located in England, Kenya, Costa Rica, Japan, Israel, India and Hong Kong. Students from the college have studied in over 75 different foreign countries.

Overseas programs for a semester or a year are open to visiting students from other colleges and universities. These students must attend a month-long orientation at the Long Island campus before they go to their selected overseas center. Students may be placed in a variety of internships and some receive stipends or room and board from the sponsoring organizations. Tuition for a semester is approximately $4,970, and room and board is about $3,000. Travel expenses, books and personal expenses are additional costs.

Requirements

Applicants should be mature and globally minded. The overseas programs usually are for college sophomores and above.

Application Procedures

There are no deadlines for application.

Contact:

> Friends World Program of Long Island University
> Johanna Klay, Admissions
> Southampton, NY 11968
> telephone (516)283-4000

GEORGETOWN UNIVERSITY

Georgetown University's Center for Immigration Policy and Refugee Assistance (CIPRA) and its Academy for Intercultural Training (AIT) offer several international internship opportunities.

Teaching English Internships

The Academy for Intercultural Training at Georgetown University coordinates internships to teach English in secondary schools, colleges and universities in a number of countries. Placements last one academic year (August or September through July) and are available in China, Indonesia, Mongolia, Egypt, the Czech and Slovak Federal Republic, Bulgaria, Poland and Hungary. The internships are offered as part of the courses "Teaching English in Asia," "Teaching English in East Central Europe," or "Teaching English in Egypt." Each course carries six graduate-level Georgetown credits. As part of each course, interns must complete a two-week orientation at Georgetown University prior to departure, write monthly field reports while abroad, and complete a written debriefing report and final research paper upon return.

The cost is $250 per credit-hour for a six-credit-hour course on teaching English. This course is held at Georgetown University two weeks prior to departure. Interns are responsible for their own room and board for this two-week period. They also are responsible for their own transportation to this course as well as round-trip airfare to the foreign country. Overseas, rooms are furnished, but not board. There is a stipend of about $225 per month.

Requirements

Applicants must have a degree from a four-year college or university. The application process consists of a written application and an interview. If accepted, interns must complete 40 hours of volunteer teaching in English as a second language prior to the orientation. Applicants for the sites in Mongolia must speak Russian. Applications are due at the beginning of March.

Development Management Internships
with Hogar de Cristo

CIPRA offers the six-credit course "Issues in Development Management," in conjunction with Hogar de Cristo, the largest charitable organization in Chile. In the Santiago area, Hogar de Cristo operates five foster homes, shelters, a hospital, a clinic and other facilities, offering the intern flexibility to work in his or her area of interest. The internships last six and one-half months and may be undertaken January-July or July-January, with an intensive two-week orientation at Georgetown prior to departure.

Most often, interns have worked in foster homes and served as role models and a source of important informal education for the children who in these homes. In addition, interns work on programs involving family interviews, intake of street children into the shelters, drug education and rehabilitation, and various other social service projects.

While in Chile, interns are responsible for sending a field report to CIPRA every two weeks. CIPRA also requires a written debriefing report and final research paper. Interns bear the cost of the course, round-trip airfare to Santiago, and medical and evacuation insurance. Hogar de Cristo provides the interns with room and board, and CIPRA contributes a small monthly stipend of about $100 for living expenses.

Requirements

Preference for these internships is given to undergraduates. The application process consists of a written application and an interview. Applicants must demonstrate proficiency in Spanish, some background in Latin America, and a commitment to social service. Applications are due in October for January placements and in April for July placements.

Application Procedures for Both Programs

To apply for these internships, request an application for the specific program or programs.

Contact for Both Programs:

Center for Immigration Policy and Refugee Assistance
Dr. Catherine A. Phee, Ph.D.
Director of Internship Programs
Georgetown University
P.O. Box 2298
Washington, D.C. 20057-1011
telephone (202)298-0229 or 298-0214

The Global Campus

The Global Campus is a program of the University of Minnesota. It organizes internships in six foreign countries through the Minnesota Studies in International Development Program (MSID). The goal of the program is to give students and professionals field experience in addressing the problems of developing countries. The internships are in Ecuador, India, Jamaica, Kenya, Morocco and Senegal. About one-third of participants are from universities and colleges other than the University of Minnesota.

The MSID program begins with fall-quarter course work at the University of Minnesota. The 10-week period includes study on development theory, cross-cultural issues, research methodology, country-specific preparation, and language training, taught by university faculty. Interns depart in January for a six-month internship. Overseas, there is a two-week orientation period that includes lectures by host-country experts in the development field, and in most sites, there is additional language preparation. Participants then are placed at their internship sites, which have been determined by in-country staff, in consultation with the faculty mentor and MSID staff. Interns are placed according to their skills, background and relevant course work. Previous interns have worked on self-help housing projects, organized recycling programs, rural nutrition programs, small business programs, and have helped to upgrade agricultural and forestry techniques. Some interns have been involved in research projects that studied female factory workers, the use of domestic pesticides, participation in village-level planning, and formal versus informal communication.

Internships are not paid. Living arrangements vary with the country, but MSID encourages homestays where they are possible. The program fee is $3,605 for each country except Senegal, the fee for which is $5,005. Interns who are not students at the University of Minnesota or the Associated Colleges of the Twin Cities should add an additional $250 to the program fees. The program fee generally includes tuition for the winter and spring quarters, internship place-ment, room and board, visa application and orientation in the host country. The program fee does not include fall-quarter tuition, room and board for the fall term, transportation to and from country site, medical insurance nor personal expenses. There is a $35 non-refundable application fee, and a non-refundable deposit is due upon acceptance into the program. The deposit is deducted from the program fee. In most instances, financial aid can be used to cover program costs. Limited scholarship assistance is available.

Requirements

Applicants must have completed at least 90 college credits and have a cumulative grade-point average of at least 2.5. They also must meet the following college-level language requirements for the designated country programs: two years of Spanish for Ecuador; two years of French for Senegal; one year of Arabic or two years of French for Morocco. It is not necessary to be a student currently in order to qualify for the program.

Application Procedures

MSID will send brochures about the internships in each country along with an application. Candidates applying by February 15 are given priority, except for placements in Kenya and Senegal. Completed applications must be received by May 15 to ensure consideration for the following year's program. If space is available, late applications will be considered through September 15.

Contact:

> MSID - The Global Campus
> 106 Nicholson Hall
> 216 Pillsbury Drive S.E.
> University of Minnesota
> Minneapolis, MN 55455
> telephone (612)626-2234
> fax (612)626-8009

The Hansard Society for Parliamentary Government was established in 1944 to study the working of parliamentary democracy and to stimulate interest in its principles. It is a British organization that offers internships for a semester in London and Oxford.

The Hansard Society's internships are intended for students of politics and public affairs who can bring to the program outstanding qualities of intelligence, initiative and responsibility. The aims of the program are to bring future leaders of the United States into sustained and active contact with the political process in Britain, and, by means of carefully selected internship placements, to enable them to meet and learn from some of its leading figures.

Hansard scholars are assigned to work as assistants to members of the House of Commons and the House of Lords, political parties, public and social policy research institutes, public affairs sections of business firms and trade union organizations, and public interest and advocacy groups. The internships are accompanied by three courses: "Modern Britain," "British Political Institutions," and a supervised research project. Grades and credits for the internships are given by Birkbeck College and are acceptable by most U.S. schools.

Fees for the program range from 3,750 to 6,300 British pounds, depending on the semester. The fee covers tuition and other aspects of the formal program, all credits and evaluations, and housing.

Requirements

Although the Hansard Scholars Programme is open to all qualified students, it is highly selective. Those majoring in political science, policy studies, economics or other social sciences, history, international relations, journalism, business administration, and other subjects concerned with political and social issues have the edge.

Application Procedures

Applicants must fill out a formal application and return it to the society with an official transcript of courses and grades.

Contact:

Dr. Lisanne Radice, Director
The Hansard Society for Parliamentary Government
16 Gowar Street
London WC1E6DP England
telephone 071-323 1131
fax 071-636 1536

ICADS *Instituto de Estudios de Desarrollo Centroamericano*
Institute for Central American Development Studies

The Institute for Central American Development Studies (ICADS) is a non-profit foundation that promotes study, research and analysis of Central American issues. The organization focuses particularly on women's issues, economic development, agricultural sciences and the environment.

ICADS offers opportunities for students to be placed as interns in Costa Rica and Nicaragua. Some examples of previous placements include: the Environmental Law Consciousness Center in San Jose, Costa Rica; a project to monitor the use of pesticides and assess their hazards; and a fishing project that trains women of a community to be more self-sufficient.

Students may enroll in semester programs that are held in the fall and the spring or they may choose the shorter summer session. A three- or four-week orientation period in San Jose, Costa Rica, begins each program. Students take Spanish, seminars on the history and politics of the region, and elective seminars. Planning and training for the internship is done during this period. The final one to two weeks is spent back at ICADS for completing the academic work. Students usually can earn about 15 credit-hours for a semester and eight credit-hours for the summer session. It is possible to enroll in consecutive sessions and be placed both in Costa Rica and Nicaragua for internships. Students live with Costa Rican or Nicaraguan families and usually have breakfast and dinner with their host families.

The program costs approximately $4,500 per semester and approximately $3,250 for the summer session. These fees cover tuition, room, partial meals, laundry service, some field trip expenses and round-trip airfare from San Jose to the internship sites. Round-trip airfare to San Jose is the responsibility of the student. Additional expenses are for books (about $50) and $90-$120 a month for lunches, local travel and personal expenses.

Requirements

These programs are open to junior and senior undergraduates and graduate students with at least one year of college Spanish. Preference is given to applicants with two or more years of college Spanish and to applicants who been involved with issues addressed by ICADS. This involvement could be participation in sanctuary activities, environmental groups, etc.

Application Procedures

Application materials are obtained directly from ICADS. Applications for the fall semester should be received before June and those for the spring should be received by mid-November. Summer applications are due April 1. Decisions usually are made within three weeks of each deadline.

Contact:

Institute for Central American Development Studies
Dept. 826
P.O. Box 025216
Miami, FL 33102-5216

The Institute of European Studies

The Institute of Asian Studies

The Institute of European Studies/-Institute of Asian Studies (IES/IAS) is a non-profit educational organization that offers undergraduates a variety of foreign study opportunities. Although it is directly affiliated and associated with approximately 100 colleges and universities, any qualified student from a four-year institution may participate. IES/IAS has program centers in Austria, England, France, Germany, Italy, Russia, Spain, Ukraine, Australia, China, Indonesia, Japan, Singapore, Taiwan and Thailand.

Internship opportunities are offered to students in the following programs: Dijon (business); London (parliamentary, business, art, communication, journalism); Nantes (teaching); Paris (business, communication, teaching); Vienna (business, teaching); and Tokyo (business). Interested students complete an internship application once accepted to the program. IES/IAS does not guarantee placement.

Housing and meals vary from program to program. For most programs, housing accommodations (family, apartment, dorm) are arranged before the student leaves the United States. In a few cases, students are expected to find their own accommodations once they arrive, with assistance from the center's staff. Depending on the program's arrangements, students might share meals with their host family, dine in the university cafeteria, or prepare meals in their own kitchen.

Tuition per semester ranges from about $5,300 to about $6,700 at European centers and from about $5,000 to about $10,350 at Asian centers. The institute publishes an annual catalog that provides detailed cost information for each of its programs.

Requirements

Applicants should be at least 18 years old and have completed four full semesters or six full quarters of actual class time by the time of participation. Students should have at least a "B" average and have taken at least one course in European or Asian Studies, such as art, business, economics, literature or politics.

Application Procedures

A preliminary application must be completed and returned to IES/IAS-Chicago with a college transcript and a non-refundable application fee of $25 for all programs other than those in Japan. The fee for the Japan programs is $60. Students meeting the preliminary requirements are sent full applications, which must be completed and returned to the institute before the program's admissions deadline. Priority deadlines are given to students from colleges and universities affiliated with the institute. Detailed admissions information can be found in the annual catalog.

Contact:

Institute of European Studies
Institute of Asian Studies
223 West Ohio Street
Chicago, IL 60610
telephone (312)944-1750
fax (312)944-1448

Ithaca College London Center

Ithaca College in Ithaca, New York, offers internships in conjunction with an academic program in London. These internships are available in the areas of international business, economics, communications, social services, politics and theater arts.

Interns work for British companies or organizations and receive academic credit of three or six credit-hours. For instance, students have been placed with members of Parliament, at the National Theater, in schools, with Radio London and with Citibank. Students keep journals and write reports that relate to their internship experiences. Interns usually work one or two days per week and use the remaining days for their courses.

Students may choose to share flats or live with a British family. Hotel rooms are reserved for the first five nights in London to allow for housing arrangements to be made. Tuition for a semester is approximately $5,100, and room and board is about $2,900.

Requirements

Applicants should be full-time undergraduates who are sophomores or above. Students must have a minimum cumulative grade-point average of 2.75 and have the approval of their adviser and dean.

Application Procedures

Submit a study-abroad program application and a college transcript. An internship application and a resume also must be submitted. Students are accepted for the London program before being selected for an internship. Placement as an intern is not guaranteed so students should have alternative course selections in mind. Upon acceptance into the program a non-refundable deposit of $250 is required.

Contact:

Ithaca College London Center
Office of International Programs
Ithaca, NY 14850
telephone (606)274-3306
fax (606)274-3474

LEHIGH UNIVERSITY

Lehigh University's Center for International Studies offers summer internships in London. The internships are in international relations and last for six weeks from early June to mid-July. Students take one course in international relations at the London School of Economics in the morning and work at a business or agency in the afternoon.

These are unpaid internships, but students receive three credit-hours for their work. British families usually provide bed and breakfast for students in the program, but students may choose other arrangements. The cost of the program is about $2,785. This includes tuition for two courses, housing, breakfasts, one-way group airfare and field trips. Additional costs are return airfare, meals other than breakfast and personal expenses. These additional expenses add up to about $1,200.

Requirements

Students who have completed one year of undergraduate study and have at least a "B-" grade-point average are eligible to apply.

Application Procedures

Application forms are due by January 15. Forms should be sent to the Office of Summer Sessions at Lehigh. A signed course pre-registration form, an essay and two passport photos should accompany the application form. Students from other schools also should include an official transcript.

Contact:

Lehigh University
Center for International Studies
Maginnes Hall #9
Bethlehem, PA 18015
telephone (215)758-4745

Lehigh University
Office of Summer Sessions
Warren Square #219
Bethlehem, PA 18015
telephone (215)758-3968

The McGeorge School of Law is part of the University of the Pacific, in Sacramento, California. It offers both summer and graduate international internship programs abroad. Placements have been made in over 30 coun-

McGeorge School of Law
University of the Pacific

tries, including Belgium, Denmark, Egypt, Hong Kong, Portugal, Spain, Sweden, Switzerland and Taiwan.

The international law internship program is offered in the fall and is open to law school graduates. The internship can be taken alone or as part of a Master of Laws in Transnational Business Practice. The program begins with six weeks of intensive training in Salzburg, Austria. Language training, laws of the host country, and general preparation to practice business and commercial law in a transnational context are the main focus of this preparation period. Interns are then placed for 10 to 12 weeks with a foreign law firm, a government office or corporate legal department. The program lasts from mid-August until mid-December. Candidates for a Master of Laws degree return to Sacramento for course work from January to June.

In most instances, interns receive a stipend that usually covers basic living costs. McGeorge School of Law helps to find housing for the interns in Salzburg, and in most cases the host firms assist the interns in finding housing for the internship period. Tuition for both the internship semester and the academic semester in Sacramento is approximately $6,720 each. Interns must pay for room, board and travel to Salzburg as well as to the site of their internship.

Requirements

Applicants must show that they have graduated from a law school approved by the American Bar Association or that they have been admitted to the bar. Foreign applicants must have graduated from a school that has the authority to issue law degrees.

Application Procedures

The first round of admissions and placements is made for applications received by January 15. Other admissions and placements are made until April 15. Submit an application, available from the Graduate Admissions Office, along with a $75 application fee, a law school transcript, evidence of a law school degree, a resume, two passport photos, and a writing sample. A statement of your interest in international law and why you wish to earn advanced certification should accompany the application. You also should have two letters of recommendation sent to the Graduate Admissions Office.

Contact:

UOP McGeorge School of Law
Graduate Admissions Office
3200 Fifth Avenue
Sacramento, CA 95817
telephone 1(800)THE-GLOBE or (916)739-7195

MOORHEAD STATE UNIVERSITY

Student Teaching Abroad (STA) is a program originated in 1969 by the Department of Education at Moorhead State University to offer future teachers the opportunity of student teaching in a foreign country. Students have been placed in about 60 countries. The program is open to all students of the Minnesota State University System and to others via cooperative arrangements with their home institutions.

Most participants are assigned to independent international schools with English as the medium of instruction, but some with special language qualifications are assigned to national schools where the instruction is in a foreign language. Others are assigned to public schools in a foreign country if English is the medium of instruction. An effort is made to place the students in geographical areas that will particularly enrich their academic backgrounds, serve their special interests and expand their cultural horizons.

Students who are not affiliated with Moorhead State University must pay a $300 placement fee. You must arrange your own air travel and living expenses, which are estimated at between $3000 and $4000. You or the school with which you are placed make housing arrangements.

Requirements

You must be a college undergraduate or graduate student. Apply about a year before you want to go.

Application Procedures

Contact the student teaching office of your college and/or Dr. Howard Freeberg at Moorhead.

Contact:

Moorhead State University
Student Teaching Abroad Program
Moorhead, MN 56560
telephone (218)236-2010

Ohio State University in Columbus, Ohio, sponsors the Ohio International Agricultural Intern Program (OIAIP). The program is to provide on-the-job training and promote interest in international exchanges in agriculture. Interns are placed in Australia, the United Kingdom and West Germany.

The program offers a long-term option that lasts for four to 12 months and a short-term option that lasts for one to three months. Interns are placed with agribusinesses that range from family farms to larger business operations. Interns might work on livestock operations, nurseries, vineyards or hop farms. Some interns live with their host families and others have separate room-and-board arrangements provided. A minimal wage is paid to cover incidental expenses. Interns are responsible for their transportation costs and health insurance.

Requirements

Applicants are usually from agricultural or horticultural colleges and universities. They should be between 19 and 30 years of age and have completed at least one year of study. It is important to have at least one year of agricultural experience. For those going to West Germany, it is important to have some knowledge of German. Only unmarried applicants are considered for internships.

Application Procedures

Applicants must submit the OIAIP application form with two letters of recommendation and a $90 application fee. This fee is refunded if you are not placed.

Contact:

Ohio State University
Ohio Agricultural Intern Program
Michael R. Crisman, Director
Room 113, 2120 Fyffe Road
Columbus, OH 43210
telephone (614)292-77720

The Partnership for Service-Learning
Academic Institutions and Service Agencies Uniting Learning and Service

The Partnership for Service-Learning is a non-profit association of colleges, universities, service and related organizations to promote community service with academic study. Students may spend up to a year studying at a foreign university and volunteering at a community service agency or project. The goal is to provide students with encounters in the real world.

Ecuador Program

The Ecuador program is in the city of Guayaquil and the course-work is at Laica University. Students usually take 12 to 15 semester-hours of college course work. Spanish, "Contemporary Ecuador" and "Institutions in Society" are required courses, but there are additional courses for those with advanced language skills. Students volunteer 20 to 25 hours per week to service programs such as teaching English as a second language, health care or economic development. This program also has internships in banking and journalism.

Room and board are provided by Ecuadoran families. The program costs approximately $3,500 per semester or summer. This includes instruction, materials sent before departure, field trips, room, board, placement and administrative fees. Individual U.S. colleges and universities may require additional fees for tuition for administration. Additional expenses include round-trip airfare, books (about $150) and personal expenses.

Requirements

This program is for undergraduates, recent college graduates or those who have deferred going to college. Applicants must be committed to fulfilling both aspects of the program. Maturity and the ability to adapt to a different culture are very important. Either two years of high-school Spanish or one year of college Spanish ia recommended.

England Program

Westminster College in Oxford is the site of Service-Learning's England program. Students begin their semester or year with a 10-day stay at the college, where they begin their academic work. The courses for this program are "Contemporary Britain," "Institutions in Society" and "Critical Reflection Through Literature and Writing." Students then begin working 35 to 40 hours per week on a community service project. Some previous opportunities have been in teaching, health care, social services or justice. Students meet at Westminster College during parts of the sixth and twelfth weeks to continue their studies, and again at the end of the program for examinations.

Westminster College provides room and most meals for the initial 10-day session. Room and board for the remaining time are arranged by the agency where the service is performed. The cost of the program is estimated at $4,000 per semester. Included in this are academic instruction, room and most meals at Westminster for the 10-day session, room and board arranged by the service agency, field trips, administrative fees and placement fees. Students are paid a stipend of $30 per week while they are in service. Additional expenses are round-trip airfare to England, books, spending money, and any fees for placement or administration charged by the U.S. college.

A summer program in England also is offered. This program lasts 10 weeks, with participants working about 40 hours per week. Students attend a three-day training session at Westminster and then are placed with service agencies. Some placements have been in probation hostels and residential homes for children or the handicapped. There is formal course work equal to nine semester-credits. Academic credit can be arranged with the U.S college or university.

Students are given stipends of about $30 per week by the service agencies. Room and board for the orientation is provided at Westminster College and by the individual agencies for the remainder of the time. The fee for the program is $3,200. Students are responsible for round-trip airfare to and from England, and will need additional spending money for personal expenses.

Requirements

Students for the semester or year program should be sophomores or above. This program is very demanding and applicants should be self-disciplined. Applicants for the summer program should be 18 years of age or older.

France Program

Montpellier, France, is the site of this program. Students may spend a semester or a full year in this Mediterranean city. They are supervised by a resident director as they work 15 to 20 hours per week and complete their academic work at the Technical Institute of the University of Montpellier. French, "French Culture," and "Institutions in Society" are required courses of study, but students with advanced French may enroll in other courses. Service may be in such areas as teaching English as a second language, day care and social services to the poor.

French families serve as hosts. Meals are with the families and at the university. The fee for one semester is approximately $4,400. Round-trip airfare, books, spending money and fees to the U.S. college are additional expenses.

Requirements

Applicants should be sophomores or above and have two years of high-school French or one year of college French. The rigorous nature of the program requires students to be motivated and self-disciplined.

Jamaica Program

Students gain insight into Jamaican history, culture, and development issues in this program. The site is Kingston and students may enroll in a summer, semester or year program. A week of orientation is followed by the start of community service and study. Students work at the service agency three days a week and then have two days of classes or field trips. Students are required to study "Jamaican/Caribbean History," "Literature of the Caribbean" and "Institutions in Society." Courses are at the College of Arts, Sciences, and Technology. Service placement is through the Caribbean Conference of Churches and has included work with the YMCA, the Human Rights Council and Girlstown School.

The cost is estimated at $3,900 for the semester program and $3,400 for the summer program. Room and board is arranged with a Jamaican family. Additional expenses are similar to those of the other Service-Learning programs.

Requirements

Students interested in the Jamaica program should be in or beyond their sophomore year of college. It is important for applicants to realize that they are serving as "good-will ambassadors."

India Program

This program is designed so that students provide help to the needy of Calcutta while they learn more about the culture of India. It is a short program that lasts for three weeks in January. Students must work at least 60 hours in one of the homes of Mother Teresa's Missionaries of Charity. They may choose to work with children, the retarded, the ill or the dying. There are 14 two-hour seminars on various aspects of Indian history, religion, and culture and 60 hours of field trips. Trips are made to other Indian cities and various points of interest.

Students can arrange to obtain three to six credit-hours worth of credit from their U.S. college or university. Credit is based on a college-level research paper due by March 1, and an evaluation given to each participant. The fee for the India program is about $2,900. Round-trip airfare from New York to Calcutta is included in this amount, along with housing, instruction, supervision, placement and evaluation. Meals are not included in the above fee and food costs total about $400. Additional money will be needed for personal expenses or shopping.

Requirements

Applicants for the India program should be college undergraduates, recent graduates or those who have deferred college admissions. It is recommended that applications be sent as early as possible since space in this program is limited.

Mexico Program

Service-Learning's Mexico program is based in Guadalajara. Students study at La Universidad Autonoma de Guadalajara for a semester or for the summer. The program begins with three weeks of practice in written and spoken Spanish, an introduction to the academic courses, and a look at the culture of Mexico. Students usually earn 12 credit-hours per semester and nine credits for the summer. Spanish and Institutions in Mexican Society are required study. Those interested in spending a year in Latin America can spend a semester or the summer in the Mexican program and then a semester or summer in the Ecuador program.

About 20 hours per week is expected to be spent in service. The three-week orientation period helps to prepare the students to serve in such areas as health or social programs for the poor, teaching, care for the elderly and working with addicts. Local families provide room and board for the participants of this program. The cost is estimated at $3,700 per semester, plus round-trip airfare, books and personal expenses. The summer program is about $3,200.

Requirements

Applicants should have at least two years of high-school Spanish or one year of college Spanish. Maturity and the ability to adapt to a different culture are desirable qualities.

Philippines Program

Trinity College near Manila gives U.S. students an opportunity to study and be involved in service with the faculty and Filipino students. A squatter's community near the campus has brought about a variety of outreach programs from the college. U.S. and Filipino students teach pre-school, tutor basic skills, sponsor a free-lunch program for children, and offer basic health care for the poor of this community. Other volunteers may serve as teacher's aides or in local hospitals. A minimum of 15 hours a week of service is required.

Students may stay for the summer, semester or year. An orientation is given upon arrival to educate the students in practical living skills in their new environment. Courses in history, sociology, economics, education, health care, literature or languages (Chinese, Tagalog or Spanish) may be taken. Six to nine credits usually are earned over the summer and 12 to 15 per semester. English is the official language of instruction for Trinity College.

Students of the program may live with local families or in the college dorm. The program costs $2,200 for the summer, $2,500 for the semester, and $4,200 for the year. Food is not covered in this amount and is approximately $7 per day. Other expenses include round-trip airfare, books and spending money.

Requirements

This program is recommended for undergraduates who are sophomores or above.

Application Procedures for All Programs

Service-Learning application forms must be sent with a $200 deposit ($250 for the India program). The applications generally are due at least eight weeks before the start of the program. Contact The Partnership for exact dates of the individual programs. Early application is urged to arrange for academic credit, service placement, visas, etc.

Contact for All Programs:

The Partnership For Service-Learning
Howard A. Berry & Linda A. Chisholm, Co-Directors
815 Second Ave., Suite 315
New York NY 10017
telephone (212)986-0989

People to People International is a non-profit, educational exchange organization founded by President Eisenhower to promote international understanding. In cooperation with the University of Missouri-Kansas City, People to People sponsors short (two to four weeks) study-abroad programs for college students. Internships in London, Dublin, Prague and other locations are offered for two months during the summer. Limited fall and spring placements also are possible.

The first week of an internship is spent in orientation and settling into life in a new country. The remaining eight weeks is spent in an unpaid work assignment with a company or public organization. The work assignments are based on information from the application and faculty recommendations. Students are required to complete a written report about their internship; graduate students may have additional work. Six credit-hours can be earned.

The program cost is about $1,775. This includes tuition, orientation, placement, mentor fees, first week's accommodations, evaluation and participation in program events. Airfare, housing for the internship period and meals are not included in the cost of the program.

Requirements

Intern applicants should be upper-level undergraduate or graduate students. Short-term seminars are offered to all undergraduate and graduate students (business, liberal arts, education, language and culture, etc.).

Application Procedures

Applications are available from People to People. A $300 deposit and two photos must accompany the completed application if applying before February 14. After February 14, the deposit plus 25 percent of the program fee balance must accompany the application. Application deadline is late April.

Contact:

People to People International
Dr. Alan M. Warne
Vice President for Programs
Collegiate Study Abroad Program
501 East Armour Boulevard
Kansas City, MO 64109
telephone (816)531-4701
fax (816)561-7502

Regent's College in London is a British college with an American-style curriculum. Rockford College in Rockford, Illinois, sponsors the Regent's College academic program and handles admissions from U.S. students. Among Regent's offerings is an Internship and Independent Study Program.

Students applying to the Internship and Independent Study Program have the option

REGENT'S COLLEGE

London

of an internship, an independent study project or a combination of the two. These internships and/or independent study projects are accompanied by other course work at Regent's for a semester or a full year. Internships are arranged with various British institutions and organizations. Some previous interns have been placed with an art gallery, a London newspaper, a British political party, Friends of the Earth, as a sound engineer at a recording studio, and with many other organizations. Interns usually work about eight to ten hours per week. The first week of each semester is reserved for student orientation. Students are assigned to learning support groups that meet every week with a tutor.

Internships are unpaid. Tuition for the program is approximately $5,400 for a semester. Room and board at Regent's College is about $2,730 per semester.

Requirements

You should be a sophomore or above and have a 2.5 grade-point average. Recommendations of faculty members at your home institution also are required. Students in the program must take an active role in planning and implementing their internships.

Application Procedures

Students first must be admitted to the Rockford College program at Regent's College. Applications and additional information are available from Regent's College.

Regent's will send you a formal application for the Internship and Independent Study Program, called a "learning contract." You and your faculty adviser at your home institution together submit the learning contract, outlining a proposal for the program. Your proposal will include a personal profile, a description of your aims, an outline of your learning objectives, how the internship will be evaluated and the amount of credit to be awarded. The learning contract then must be submitted to Regent's College in London. Contracts for the fall semester should be received before May 15 and for the spring semester by November 15.

Contact:

Regent's College
c/o Rockford College
Rockford, IL 61108
telephone (815)226-3376
fax (815)226-4119

Academic Dean
Regent's College
Inner Circle, Regent's Park
London NW1 4NS England
fax 44 71 487-7425

Saint Clare's is an independent international college in Oxford, England. It offers a liberal arts program for students from the United States and other countries who wish to spend a semester or more in England.

Students may participate in internships with the approval of their home institution and of St. Clare's. Internships are available in local schools, the University Museum and in local industry. Students usually take five courses with the internship counting as one course.

St. Clare's will arrange for housing in a bed-and-breakfast situation or a room with cooking privileges. Students who wish an apartment or to share a house must make their own arrangements. Housing, food, personal expenses and local travel are approximately $180 per week. Tuition is about $4,490 for the semester or $8,980 for the year.

Requirements

Students from American colleges and universities should have at least a 2.5 grade-point average and be a sophomore or above. All students must have formal permission from their home institution before they will be considered for admission.

Application Procedures

St. Clare's can give additional information on the internships and can supply the application for the liberal arts program. Send the completed application with your course choices, a letter from your school approving the choices, a reference from a faculty member, a current transcript and a $50 registration fee.

Contact:

St. Clare's
Liberal Arts Programme
139 Banbury Road
Oxford OX 2 7AL, England
telephone Oxford (865)52031

DIVISION OF INTERNATIONAL PROGRAMS ABROAD

Syracuse University offers several opportunities for summer internships abroad. Students going to London are able to gain practical work experience in fashion design, management or law. In Geneva, internships in international studies are available, and in Strasbourg, students have the opportunity to work for the Council of Europe. Students earn three to six credit-hours for the internships.

These programs are for upper-level undergraduate or graduate students and last for about six weeks. The program fees and tuition for each program vary from about $3,700 to $4,300. The cost includes tuition for six credit-hours of course work, housing, field trips and program activities. For some of the programs, round-trip transportation and at least some meals also are covered. A limited number of small grants are available to students able to demonstrate need.

Requirements

Students should be upper-level undergraduate or graduate students. Most of the internships require advanced work in a specific area of study. Some of the internships require basic French or German. Syracuse University publishes a yearly brochure about its summer programs abroad and the individual requirements for each program.

Application Procedures

Syracuse University has additional information on the specific internships and can supply application materials. A non-refundable application fee of $35 must accompany the completed application. Applications for these summer programs generally are due either March 1 or March 15.

Contact:

> Syracuse University
> Division of International Programs Abroad
> 119 Euclid Avenue
> Syracuse, NY 13244
> telephone (315)443-3471

The University of Pennsylvania

The University of Pennsylvania organizes summer internships in France and Poland. The program in France is run in cooperation with the l'Universite de Technologie de Compiegne. The program in Poland is offered in conjunction with the Warsaw School of Economics.

The program in France combines a study program with a two-week internship with a French business, while the intern lives with a French family. The main goal of the program in Poland is to acquaint students with the social, economic and political problems of the country as it moves from a totalitarian to a democratic system. Classroom instruction is complemented by short-term internships with Polish or joint-venture organizations.

Cost for the program in France is $2,200 for tuition and $1,200 for room, board and activities. You must pay for your own transportation. Cost for the program in Poland is $2,150 for tuition and $100 for housing. Again, you must pay for your own transportation.

Requirements

Students should be highly motivated, flexible and able to withstand the everyday stresses and strains of coping with a different culture and environment.

Application Procedures

Application deadline for both programs is March 1. Your application must be accompanied by a non-refundable fee of $25 for processing. On admission you must send a non-refundable $200 deposit to hold a place—this will be credited toward the final cost of the program.

Contact:

Penn Summer Abroad
College of General Studies
University of Pennsylvania
3440 Market Street, Suite 100
Philadelphia, PA 19104-3335
telephone (215)898-5738

UNIVERSITY OF
ROCHESTER

The University of Rochester sponsors internships in several European countries. The internship program is in cooperation with the non-profit agency Educational Programmes Abroad. Internships are available is London, Brussels, Bonn/Cologne, Madrid and Paris.

London Internships

Students have a wide range of internships in London from which to choose. There are internships in British politics, museums, health sciences and medical research, business and theater.

British politics interns work as assistants to members of Parliament, in law offices, for pressure groups, at political party headquarters, in constituency offices, etc. Students who intern with members of the European Parliament may travel to Brussels or Strasbourg for up to 10 days with all their expenses paid. Interns also have been placed in a wide variety of museums and galleries in London. These include the British Film Institute, the Museum of London, the National Maritime Museum and the National Museum of Earth Science. The interns are involved in research, preparing exhibits, recording and cataloging. For students interested in health care or medical research, there are internships in hospitals associated with the University of London. Health care internships can provide experience in hospital administration, nutrition, health education, occupational therapy, physical therapy, etc. Medical research interns work in laboratories or teaching hospitals.

The theater internships are in small "fringe" theaters, similar to off-Broadway theaters. Students work as general assistants and are involved in all aspects of theatrical production. Business interns have been placed in banking, advertising, public relations, accounting, marketing, personnel and publishing.

Semester interns usually work three or four days per week and take two courses associated with their internship. Interns for the spring quarter and the summer session only take the internship. During an orientation period, students are housed together and learn more about the program, their internship and living in London. After the orientation period, students may live with a British family or share an apartment with other interns.

The London semester costs approximately $6,200. This includes tuition, fees and housing. For students staying with a British family, some meals will be included in the cost. The spring quarter (early April to mid-June) and the summer session (early June to mid-August) costs about $3,500 for those seeking University of Rochester credits and about $2,700 for those who do not want credit from the university. These fees include tuition, fees, housing and some meals.

Brussels Internships

... in politics, business or with special
int ... to four days per week and
ta ... the spring quarter
w ... courses.
" ... ne of the

ers of the
s will make
n research,
etings. Some
ire advanced

n move to their
n an apartment.
quarter is $3,500
for ... $2,700 for others.
These costs ... meals.

Bonn/Cologne ... s

Internships in Bonn or Cologne are ... in politics, the arts, health science, business and medical research. All of the internships require proficiency in German. Five semesters of college German is the minimal requirement. Students work three to four days per week and take two courses related to their internship. This program is for a semester or the spring quarter (early April to mid-June).

Interns interested in politics are placed in the offices of members of the Bundestag, the federal parliament of Germany. Their duties include research, handling correspondence, attending meetings and dealing with constituency problems. Some internships also are available with lobby groups. Museums in Bonn and Cologne have a variety of internships and the Cologne Opera lets students work as general assistants. The health science internships are especially for psychology and sociology majors. Students are placed at the Public Research Institute in Bonn and at various health, youth and immigrant centers. Medical research interns have been placed at the Institute of Pathology in Cologne.

The orientation period is two weeks for the semester program and one week for the spring quarter. There are four weeks of intensive language training for most students before the internship begins. Those who demonstrate their proficiency in German may begin their internship right after the orientation. Students may choose to live with a German family or to live independently. This program costs about $6,150 for a semester and $2,700-$3,500 for the spring quarter.

Madrid Internships

The Madrid internships are available in politics, business, the media and in art museums. Interns work three to four days per week and all interns need a high degree of proficiency in Spanish.

Interns in politics work as research and administrative assistants to members of the Cortes (the legislative body), refugee offices, political party headquarters or international law offices. Business interns have been placed in retail stores, computer companies, a record company and travel agencies. Media placements have been with television stations and press agencies.

A two-week orientation is held on the campus of the Universidad Complutense de Madrid. Interns who are proficient in Spanish may begin there internship after the orientation, others may take language orientation sessions before beginning their internships. Students may choose from among several living arrangements while in Madrid: a homestay with a Spanish family; a rented room that provides a continental breakfast; a dormitory where students prepare their own meals; or independent living arrangements. The Madrid program costs about $6,250 for tuition, fees, housing and some meals.

Paris Internships

In Paris, there are opportunities for internships in politics, business, the media, the theater, museums and the social sciences. Interns in politics have been placed with the Assemblee Nationale, local Paris councils, political party headquarters and political pressure groups. Interns need at least five semesters of college French to qualify for the program.

The Paris program lasts for a full year. During the fall semester, students take courses at the L'Ecole Europeenne des Affaires (EAP). Courses in management studies, politics, history, economics, architecture, business and the arts are offered. Students take French classes and concentrate on spoken French. For the spring semester, students take an internship and continue their academic work. The first two weeks of the fall semester is spent in orientation. All students are housed together for this period. Three hours each day is devoted to language orientation and the remainder of the time is spent in cross-cultural training, field trips and seminars. Students may choose a homestay with a French family, a student dormitory, or an independent apartment. The cost for the year is approximately $15,500. This amount includes tuition, fees, housing and some meals.

Requirements

Applicants should be college juniors and seniors with at least a 3.0 grade point average. Recent graduates or graduate students are considered for the internships in Bonn, Brussels, Madrid and the summer session in London. The programs in Bonn, Brussels and Madrid have language proficiency requirements.

Application Procedures

Applications are available from the University of Rochester. The application deadlines are: October 31, for the spring semester; March 31, for the spring quarter, and April 1, for the summer and fall sessions.

Contact:

University of Rochester
Study Abroad Office
312 Lattimore Hall
Rochester, NY 14627
telephone (716)275-2354

THE WASHINGTON CENTER

For Internships and Academic Seminars

The Washington Center for Internships and Academic Seminars is a placement agency that finds internship programs in Washington for students with a particular interest. International organizations and embassies are among the placements.

Internships are for fall, winter, spring or summer. They are combined with weekly courses and are for academic credit.

Students pay a program fee of just under $2,000 and a housing fee of $1,500. Scholarships are available to those who qualify.

Requirements

To participate in the internship program, you must be a second-semester sophomore or above at the time you attend, with at least a 2.5 grade-point average on a 4.0 scale.

Application Procedures

Write the center for an application brochure.

Contact:

The Washington Center for Internships
and Academic Seminars
514 Tenth Street, N.W.
Suite 600
Washington, D.C. 20004
telephone (202)624-8000

WISC

The Washington International Studies Center

The Washington International Studies Center (WISC) offers a London Internship Program in the fall, spring and summer. It also offers a Washington Summer Internship Program.

London Internship Program

For students who wish to intern and study in London, WISC offers in association with the Hansard Society for Parliamentary Government a distinguished academic internship program in public policy. Selected students admitted as Hansard scholars enroll in three courses taught by the Politics and Sociology Department of Birkbeck College, University of London. These are "Modern Britain," "British Political Institutions" and a supervised research project. Students are placed in supervised internships with members of the House of Commons, political parties, etc. Hansard Scholars who complete the program are recommended for 15 U.S. semester-credits from Birkbeck College.

WISC quotes its fees for each semester as about 3,500 British pounds, payable to the Hansard Society. Fees include tuition and housing, but not meals.

See our entry under "Hansard Society for Parliamentary Government," which appears earlier in this section.

Requirements

You must be an undergraduate or graduate student. There is no grade-point average recommended, but placements are competitive.

Washington Summer Internship Program

The Washington Summer Internship Program consists of a research internship, one or two lecture courses, guest lectures, educational tours and on-site visits. Four semester-credits will be recommended to a home college for a research internship and two credits for each lecture course. Students choose one or two lecture courses for two credits each. It is up to the home college or university to award a student credit. The internship is held with a government agency, a Senate or

House office, a think tank, a newspaper or magazine, a lobbying group or an economic organization. International organizations are among those participating.

The program fee is under $4,000. It includes tuition for six to eight credits, housing and other facilities (gym, pool, library, etc.) at a major Washington University, weekly buffet dinners with guest speakers, at least two discussion lunches with policy-makers or journalists, educational tours and other activities that include access to a large weekend house at Rehoboth Beach. There is a $100 damage/security deposit.

Requirements

You must be an advanced-level high-school student or an undergraduate student. No grade-point average is recommended, but placements are highly competitive.

Application Procedures for Both Programs

Submit WISC's application with a recommendation from a faculty member, a current transcript, a 100-word statement on your goals and why you wish to enroll, and a non-refundable application fee of $35. Applicants who are college students also should include a resume. Write the center for a brochure and application.

Contact for Both Programs:

The Washington International Studies Center
214 Massachusetts Avenue, N.E., Suite 450
Washington, D.C. 20002
telephone (202)547-3275

Section III

**Independent
Internships
and
Traineeships**

*This section lists international internship oppor-
tunities not tied to an academic program, both
paid and unpaid. The list includes opportunities
both in the United States and abroad.*

The Africa Fund (AF) and the American Committee on Africa (ACOA) are two separate organizations concerned with a number of issues in southern Africa, including protection of human rights and ending apartheid. ACOA organizes programs and projects to bring these issues before the American people and to build support. AF works with ACOA in developing a better understanding of African issues in the United States. It also provides relief to African refugees through shipments, grants and emergency aid.

ACOA and AF sponsor an internship program for students. Interns are for the most part volunteers, as ACOA/AF does not offer salaries or stipends adequate to cover living expenses. Since the two organizations share offices and staff, interns work with both organizations, assuming responsibility for regular office functions such as monitoring and clipping publications, answering telephones, directing use of the research center, photocopying, participating in staff meetings, and assisting in production of reports and publications. Interns often take on individual projects, depending on their backgrounds and capabilities and the needs of the organizations.

Requirements

There are no special requirements for application. It is recommended that applicants have a work or academic background in fields relating to Africa or issues affecting African development, have a strong interest in ACOA/AF programs and have a commitment to hard work. Many students accepted into the program are affiliated with a college work-study program.

Application Procedures

Request an application from ACOA/AF by sending a letter and your resume. There are no deadlines for application. Interns can begin work at any time throughout the year for any duration of time. Students applying for the summer months should send in completed applications by the beginning of April.

Contact:

The American Committee on Africa & the Africa Fund
Research Director
198 Broadway
New York, NY 10038

THE AFRICAN-AMERICAN INSTITUTE

The African-American Institute was founded in 1953 to strengthen relations between the United States and Africa by encouraging U.S. participation in the development of Africa. Primary activities include designing and implementing manpower training programs for private and government organizations in Africa and the United States; sponsoring conferences for policy-makers; conducting visitor programs; and providing information and services to individuals and companies involved in trade or investment in Africa.

The African-American Institute sponsors a year-round student intern program for post-graduate students at its office in Washington, D.C. While interns are not paid, academic credit usually can be arranged through the school or college. Specific duties vary greatly and are largely dependent upon the capabilities of the intern.

Africa Report, a publication of the African-American Institute, also uses interns at its New York City office. Interns are unpaid and usually work at least two days a week for a semester, or full time for a summer. Interns help in monitoring a very large library of news clippings as well as in laying out and binding news files. They may contribute short articles to the "Update" section of the magazine. Qualified interns might move into other areas of work, such as editing, proofreading and layout.

Requirements

Applicants should have a background or strong interest in African affairs and be able to demonstrate organizational and writing skills. Proficiency in the French language also is helpful.

Those applying for an internship with *Africa Report* should have an interest in Africa and learning about magazine publication. They should have good writing skills, be accurate and work well with details.

Application Procedures

For the Washington, D.C., internships send a resume, writing sample and two letters of recommendation three months before the date you'll be available for work.

Contact:

(for the Washington, D.C., internships)
The African-American Institute
Ms. Annie J. Corboy, Director
Constituency Development
1625 Massachusetts Ave., NW, Suite 210
Washington, D.C. 20036
telephone (202)265-6332

(for the *Africa Report* internships)
Africa Report
Daphne Topouzis, Assistant Editor
833 United Nations Plaza
New York, NY 10017
telephone (212)949-5666
fax (212)286-9493

African Council on Communication Education
Le Conseil Africain d'Enseignement de la Communication

The African Council of Communication Education (ACCE) is an institution that is involved in communication, education, development and support throughout Africa. It is headquartered in Nairobi, Kenya.

Internships with ACCE last for one year and have been available in the areas of communication research and accounting. Interns usually help support ACCE programs in training, research, documentation and publication. They also might help with administrative duties. Interns also may attend seminars in other parts of Africa. Interns receive a stipend of $300 per month and ACCE helps to find housing. Previous interns have arranged college credit through their home college or university.

Requirements

You should be a college graduate or graduate student. ACCE prefers that your undergraduate degree be in communication and that you have an interest in Africa.

Application Procedures

Submit your resume with a cover letter at any time.

Contact:

African Council on Communication Education
Batilloi Warritay
University of Nairobi
Education Building, Third Floor
P.O. Box 47495
Nairobi, Kenya

 **Africare**

Africare was established in 1971 by U.S. and African citizens concerned about drought conditions in Africa. It is a private, non-profit organization that seeks to help strengthen rural sectors and protect the environment, as well as to provide emergency assistance to African nations in crisis situations. It currently is involved in over 200 development programs in 23 nations.

Africare's internship program is primarily domestic. Interns are assigned to the organization's Washington, D.C., headquarters. They are not paid and must be able to maintain themselves in the Washington, D.C., metropolitan area with little assistance from Africare. Opportunities exist for both undergraduate and graduate students.

Requirements

Undergraduate college students must be enrolled currently in an accredited college or university, with an academic or technical course background related to African and/or international development, preferably with concentration in the area of agriculture, health, forestry or water resources.

Graduate students must have current or pending enrollment in an accredited university and be graduates of an accredited college or university with a technical or academic degree in agriculture, forestry, health, water resources, international development or related field.

Interns are expected to have good working habits, motivation, excellent research and writing skills, a willingness to learn and a sincere interest in Africa and African development.

Application Procedures

Send a letter of application explaining the reason for seeking an internship with Africare, a resume and one-page summary stating your specific interests and concerns regarding development in Africa.

Contact:

Africare
Dr. Joseph C. Kennedy,
Director of International Development
440 R Street, NW
Washington, D.C. 20001
telephone (202)462-3614

AFS INTERCULTURAL PROGRAMS

AFS Intercultural Programs is an international, non-profit organization that promotes intercultural learning through worldwide exchange programs involving students, host families, teachers and volunteers. AFS stands for the American Field Service, which was founded by volunteer ambulance drivers shortly after the outbreak of World War I. It since has become a people-to-people movement that aims to transcend national, social, racial, political and religious barriers and promotes intercultural learning with exchange programs for people of all ages. It encompasses over 50 countries and links over 100,000 volunteers and 30,000 participants the world over through ideas, experiences and humanitarian ideals.

The headquarters for the AFS Intercultural Programs in New York City has a college internship program that was started in 1985. Students are recruited primarily from the greater New York area. To date, over 170 students have participated in the program.

The purpose of the internship program is to enhance the experiences of students in their specialized study areas while providing AFS departments with additional human resources. Internships involve assignments in area studies, international program administration, research in intercultural learning, finance, marketing, public relations, publications, fund raising, personnel, program support, etc. While students are invited to submit general applications for positions, from time to time AFS publicizes specific internship assignments. Notification of these specific assignments is sent to the offices of career services or cooperative education at various colleges and universities. The information also is available upon request from AFS's personnel department.

Internships are offered in the spring (January-June), summer (June-August), and fall (September-January). They are part-time during the fall and spring semesters and full-time during the summer. College work-study is available to some students.

Generally, interns are unpaid, unless AFS has signed a contract with his/her college for a work-study program. AFS provides all interns with a stipend for lunch ($5.00 per work day of five hours or more) in its cafeteria, plus daily transportation to and from AFS.

Requirements

Interns must be college sophomores, juniors, seniors or graduate students with a minimum grade-point average of 2.5, and must have good academic standing with their college. Students should be living or attending colleges in the New York area or its surroundings. Out-of-town students may apply if they have housing in the vicinity.

Selection is based on applications submitted, interviews and references. Students should have some knowledge or interest in intercultural/international studies, although it is not necessary.

Application Procedures

AFS will send you an application for internship. Application may be made directly to AFS or through school internship or career services offices.

Contact:

Internship Program Coordinator
AFS Intercultural Programs
Personnel Department
313 East 43rd Street
New York, NY 10017
telephone (212)949-4242

The Aries Group, Ltd.

The Aires Group carries out consulting activities in the areas of financial systems assessment; development of financial institutions, instruments and markets; private-sector development; and privatization of state-owned enterprises in developing countries. It recently has been involved in projects in Asia, the Pacific, Central America, Africa and the Middle East.

The Aires Group hires interns to work in its headquarters in Crystal City, Virginia, just outside Washington, D.C., for periods usually in excess of two months. Interns are paid an hourly wage determined by their abilities. Duties include research, word processing/data entry and preparation of reports.

Requirements

Professionals who work with Aires tend to have backgrounds in banking, securities, accounting, law and economics. Applicants for internships should be college undergraduate or graduate students, or recent graduates, with majors in business, economics, political science or international relations.

Application Procedures

Send a letter of application, indicating date of availability, with a resume and two letters of recommendation.

Contact:

The Aires Group, Ltd.
Mr. Anthony Costanzo, Vice President, Projects
1745 Jefferson Davis Highway, Suite 404
Arlington, VA 22202
telephone (703)892-9123

AMERICAN BAR ASSOCIATION   Section of International Law and Practice

The American Bar Association sponsors an International Legal Exchange (ILEX) program for lawyers. Under this program, law firms in foreign countries host American lawyers usually for one to six months. The program also allows foreign lawyers to work in the United States for up to six months. The goal of the program is to enhance the understanding of legal systems in foreign countries as well as to allow foreign lawyers to learn more about the U.S. legal system.

Not all of the positions have a salary or stipend, so participants may be responsible for living expenses while overseas. Extensions sometimes can be arranged with the host law firm.

Requirements

The ILEX program is open to U.S. and foreign lawyers. Proficiency in the language of the host country is recommended.

Application Procedures

Submit a completed application, recent photo, two references, a statement of purpose and an application fee of $200. This fee is non-refundable. All application materials should be received at least six months before the desired starting date. Application materials can be obtained from the American Bar Association.

Contact:

> American Bar Association
> International Legal Exchange Program
> Edison W. Dick, Executive Director
> 1700 Pennsylvania Ave., N.W.
> Suite 620
> Washington, D.C. 20006
> telephone (202)393-7122
> fax (202)347-9015

american friends service committee

The American Friends Service Committee (AFSC) is a Quaker organization that carries on a variety of educational, humanitarian and social-change programs. The organization administers the Quaker United Nations office in New York City, where interns serve for one year. It also sponsors summer service opportunities in Latin America and the Caribbean.

Quaker United Nations Office

The Quaker United Nations Office (QUNO) represents all Quaker groups worldwide and seeks to inform its constituents as well as present their views to United Nations officials. The office focuses on disarmament and security matters, social and human rights issues, and issues of economic justice.

Interns serve from September to August and provide program support for QUNO staff. Approximately 15 hours per week is spent in general office tasks. Interns also might do research, monitor an issue of interest, assist with a monthly newsletter or be involved in outreach programs. A grant of about $210 per week covers living expenses in New York City. AFSC provides medical insurance and can assist in finding housing.

Requirements

These internships are for recent college graduates who are interested in international affairs and international development.

Application Procedures

Submit the QUNO internship application along with a cover letter, a curriculum vita and four references. A one- or two-page writing sample that details a particular concern or area of interest to you within the focus of the organization is required. The application deadline is mid-April.

Contact:

Quaker United Nations Office FWCC/AFSC
777 United Nations Plaza
New York, NY 10017
telephone (212)682-2745

Summer Community Service in Mexico

AFSC has been sponsoring short-term community-service projects in Latin America since 1939. Most of the projects are in Mexico, but occasionally they are in other Latin American countries. Volunteers may find themselves constructing or repairing schools, houses, roads and the like. Other projects also have involved reforestation, gardening, health and nutrition.

Volunteers live and work in rural communities usually from late June to mid-August. They are placed in groups at each project site. Each project has two leaders with half the group being from Latin America and the other half from the United States. The group chooses a project based on the skills available and the needs of the community where they will be working. The project group usually lives in a school or unused building. The group shares in all project tasks, housekeeping and shopping. They also try to participate in the life of the village as much as possible.

Volunteers attend orientation conferences before the projects and an evaluation session for all groups is held after the six-week work period. A $700 fee covers orientation, food, lodging, transportation during the project, and insurance. Volunteers must pay for their own transportation to Mexico, a required health examination, inoculations and personal expenses.

Requirements

Applicants should be 18 to 26 years of age and be in good health. They should be able to adapt well to group living and to rural village life. Volunteers must be willing to respect local social customs and organizations. Spanish is required since it is the primary language of communication. Other useful skills are experience in construction, gardening, arts, crafts, child care and recreation.

Cuba Summer Program

The Cuba Summer Program is organized and hosted by the Cuban Baptist Worker-Student Committee (COEBAC). AFSC has recruited and sent young people to this program since 1981. After a two-day orientation in Miami, participants spend three weeks in work camps in Cuba. Most of the work is on small farms near Havana where they help with sugar cane and other crops. Participants also attend the COEBAC Youth Conference during the final week of the program. They may be asked to give presentations in Spanish at the conference or to participate in services at local Baptist churches. A fee of $250 covers administrative costs, food and lodging in Miami for the orientation. Food and lodging in Cuba are supplied by the host organization. Participants are responsible for all round-trip transportation costs to Miami and Cuba.

Requirements

Applicants should be 18 to 28 years of age, mature, open-minded, interested in Cuba and fluent in Spanish. Community activist or church volunteer experience is helpful.

Application Procedures for Mexico and Cuba Programs

AFSC can provide application materials for the Mexico and Cuba programs. An essay is required for the Mexico program; it should discuss the applicant's experience, expectations and motivation for becoming part of a project. The application deadline for both programs is June 1.

Contact for Mexico and Cuba Programs:

American Friends Service Committee
Personnel Department
1501 Cherry Street
Philadelphia, PA 19102
telephone (215)241-7295

The American Jewish Congress was founded in 1918 to defend the rights of Jews throughout the world. The organization fights anti-Semitism and all forms of racism.

Legislative interns work at the office of the Washington representative of the congress. Interns may attend and report on U.S. congressional committee meetings and hearings or interest-group meetings on numerous policy issues. The American Jewish Congress is involved in such issues as women's rights, nuclear disarmament, Israel and the Middle East, separation of church and state, and civil rights. Duties also might include such tasks as filing news articles and mailings.

Internships are offered three times a year, at approximately the times of the semester and summer sessions of most colleges. All positions are voluntary and the length of internships is very flexible. Interns must work at least 10 hours during the school year and full time during the summer. The Jewish American Congress helps interns receive college credit for their service.

Requirements

Undergraduate, graduate, or postgraduate students may apply. Applicants should have majors in political science, international relations, public administration, Judaic studies, domestic affairs or other related fields.

Application Procedures

Send the application with a resume and a brief writing sample.

Contact:

American Jewish Congress
Office of the Washington Representative
Art Rublin, Internship Coordinator
2027 Massachusetts Ave., N.W.
Washington, D.C. 20036
telephone (202)332-4001

The American-Scandinavian Foundation

The American-Scandinavian Foundation (ASF) is a non-profit organization founded in 1910 to develop and promote educational and cultural exchanges between the United States and the five Scandinavian countries of Denmark, Finland, Iceland, Norway and Sweden. ASF places American college students and recent graduates in short-term "training" programs with Scandinavian employers. While the interns or "trainees" are responsible for their own airfare, they receive salaries sufficient to cover living costs for the period of training.

Short-term assignments range from eight to 12 weeks up to six months. Positions are available in Scandinavia for students in engineering, chemistry, computer science/COBOL application, agriculture, horticulture and forestry. Application deadline is December 15 for summer/fall placements.

Requirements

Applicants should be full-time students in the relevant field of study with three years of undergraduate studies completed and some type of related work experience. Knowledge of a Scandinavian language is not required.

These requirements do not apply to someone who has located work through his or her own business or personal contacts. In such a case, ASF can help the individual obtain the necessary work permit. All ASF needs is a copy of the correspondence with the Scandinavian firm, confirming you've been offered a temporary position that will provide an income adequate to cover living expenses.

Application Procedures

Send a resume and letter of application, specifying the exact field and country in which you wish to train, and mention the skills you have that would be attractive to a potential employer. ASF will evaluate your resume and determine your chances for placement. If placement seems likely, ASF will forward an application. You then must complete the application and mail it in with a processing fee of $50.

Contact:

The American-Scandinavian Foundation
ATTN: Exchange Division
725 Park Avenue
New York, NY 10021
telephone (212)879-9779

ASTA

The American Society of Travel Agents (ASTA) is the largest travel-trade association in the world. It serves almost 21,000 members in 121 countries. Members tend to be from independent travel agencies, hotels, car rental firms, rail lines, cruise lines and airlines. ASTA serves as an information resource and promotes ethical business practices in the travel industry worldwide.

ASTA sponsors four to six interns once a year in September/October, during the World Travel Congress it holds for its members. The event lasts one week, with seminars scheduled for three days, a large trade show for three days and general sessions most every day. Locations during the past few years included Rome, Singapore, Budapest, Houston and Miami.

Interns receive room and board at the hotel where the Congress is held and all transportation costs in exchange for serving as administrative staff during the week. Some travel schools also offer academic credit to students who work as interns. General duties include helping to set up seminar rooms, helping to register members, collecting evaluations, distributing handouts, assisting speakers and so on.

Requirements

Applicants must be travel industry students at a travel school or college with a travel and tourism program, and have at least a 3.0 grade-point average.

Application Procedures

Applications are sent to all ASTA-member travel schools in the spring. You must send in a transcript and two recommendations along with the completed application. You also must complete a project as part of the application. Deadline is usually mid-June. Students who are attending non-ASTA-member travel schools are eligible to apply, but must write to ASTA and request an application.

Contact:

American Society of Travel Agents
Education Department
1101 King Street
Alexandria, VA 22314
telephone (703)739-2782 ext. 608

AMNESTY INTERNATIONAL USA

Amnesty International is an independent organization that works for the release of all prisoners of conscience. The group works for fair trials for political prisoners and seeks an end to the inhumane treatment of prisoners.

Internships

Amnesty International USA has five regional offices that oversee the operations of the group in this country. The regional offices have opportunities for full-time and part-time interns. The full-time positions are for 35 hours per week and last one year, usually August to September. The positions are paid, but the pay covers only expenses. Interns in these positions frequently coordinate various programs for the organization. The part-time positions are unpaid and may last a semester or more. These interns are expected to work at least 20 hours per week and usually are able to arrange academic credit. Duties might include coordinating the work of others, initiating projects, and necessary clerical duties.

CARL A. RUDISILL LIBRARY
LENOIR-RHYNE COLLEGE

Requirements

Applicants for internships should be able to work well with a team, as well as independently. They should have good writing skills, good oral communication, computer experience and good organization skills. It is important for applicants to know the work of Amnesty International and be familiar with international human rights issues. Full-time interns must be college graduates.

The Ralph J. Bunch Human Rights Fellowship Program

This fellowship, named after the 1950 Nobel Peace Prize recipient, is designed to strengthen leadership abilities. Another goal is to establish better ties between Amnesty International and ethnic groups and organizations.

Participants receive intensive training in international human rights. They must serve a 10-month residency in a regional office of Amnesty International. The full-time commitment is to a special project that fits the needs of the regional office and the interests of the participant. One fellow organized a city-wide, human rights art contest and another organized Amnesty International chapters at African-American colleges.

A stipend and travel expenses are paid. Academic credit can be arranged for students serving as fellows.

Requirements

Applicants must be members of American minority groups such as Africans, Arabs, Asians, Latinos and Native Americans. College undergraduate or graduate students may apply. Some experience in human rights work is desirable. A good academic record and good organization and communication skills also are very important.

Application Procedures

To apply for an internship, send an application with a resume and a writing sample. Early application is suggested. Acceptance decisions usually are made in November for the winter and spring interns; April or May for the summer interns; and in June or August for the fall interns.

Applicants for the Human Rights Fellowship should contact the regional office nearest their home or school for more information about the positions. Applications for the fellowships are due by March 15.

Contact for Both Programs:

Amnesty International USA
Mid-Atlantic Regional Office (DE, MD, PA, VA, DC, WV)
1118 22nd Street, NW
Washington, D.C. 20037
telephone (202)775-5161

Mid-West Regional Office (IL, IN, IA, KS, KY, MI, MN, MO, NE, ND, OH, SD, WI)
53 West Jackson, Room 1162
Chicago, IL 60604
telephone (312)427-2060

Northeast Regional Office (CT, ME, MA, NH, NJ, NY, RI, VT)
58 Day Street
Somerville, MA 02144
telephone (617)623-0202

Southern Regional Office (AL, AR, FL, GA, LA, MS, NC, OK, SC, TN, TX)
740 West Peachtree
Atlanta, GA 30308
telephone (404)876-5661

Western Regional Office (AK, AZ, CA, CO, HI, MT, NV, NM, OR, UT, WA, WY)
3407 W, 6th Street, #704
Los Angeles, CA 90020
telephone (213)388-1237

TheAsia Foundation

The Asia Foundation is a non-profit organization established in 1954 to lend American assistance to Asians and Pacific Islanders for the growth and development of their societies, to promote regional cooperation, and to further Asian-American understanding, cooperation and friendship.

The foundation offers internships at its San Francisco headquarters in its Center for Asian Pacific Affairs, public affairs, programs, and its Regional/Luce Scholars Program. Internships vary from four to five weeks up to 12 weeks. Responsibilities range from monitoring periodicals to compiling databases, to providing administrative support, to writing, editing and producing newsletters, brochures and annual reports. Weekly hours required of interns range from eight to 37.5. Each intern is paid an hourly wage of $4.25.

Requirements

Requirements vary according to the position. All positions require good communication and organization skills. Several positions require computer literacy (WordPerfect preferred). The internship under the Center For Asian Pacific Affairs requires a degree and/or a major in political science, history, economics or international affairs. A journalism major is preferred for the public affairs internship.

Application Procedures

You must complete an application form, attach a resume and cover letter and send it to the attention of the Personnel Officer at the below address.

Contact:

The Asia Foundation
Personnel Officer
P.O. Box 193223
San Francisco, CA 94119-3223
telephone (415)982-4640
fax (415)392-8863

The Association for International Practical Training (AIPT) is a private, non-profit organization dedicated to encouraging and facilitating the exchange of qualified individuals between the United States and other countries so that they may gain practi-cal work experience and improve international understanding. In collaboration with similar groups around the world, AIPT assists with on-the-job practical training opportunities for professionals and students in a wide variety of fields. AIPT sponsors exchanges with Australia, Finland, France, Ireland, Japan, Malaysia, the Netherlands, Switzerland, the United Kingdom and Germany. Working knowledge of the host country's language is required in most cases.

The specific fields of training available in a given country are determined by the cooperating organization in that country. AIPT administers three programs of exchange: student exchanges, hotel/culinary exchanges and career development exchanges. Applicants to the career development exchanges must locate a host employer willing to offer them a training program. Applicants to the student exchanges program or the hospitality/tourism exchanges program may either find their own host employer or become an "open" applicant for whom AIPT will attempt to locate a training placement.

In an open application, AIPT will contact its counterpart organization in the other country, which will endeavor to locate a suitable assignment with training that will be of mutual benefit to both the trainee and employer. Open applications cannot be processed for all countries and all industries; contact AIPT to determine whether the country and industry in which you are interested allows for open applications. On the average, four to six months is required to locate a suitable placement. If AIPT agrees to assist an individual in locating a training placement, the application can be active for one year with the possibility of placement in one of two countries selected by the applicant. Once an employer has agreed to accept an applicant, the terms and conditions of the training assignment are forwarded to he applicant. The individual is required to accept or decline the offer within three weeks of receipt. Upon acceptance, a program fee may be charged by the counterpart organization and usually is the responsibility of the trainee.

The process for reserved applications is fairly straightforward and must always start with the approval of your application by AIPT. On approval, your application will be sent to the appropriate AIPT counterpart organization in the country of your choosing, and further contact then will be made between the counterpart and your prospective employer in that country. A program fee may be charged by the counterpart organization and is usually the responsibility of the employer.

The employer is required to provide a maintenance allowance sufficient to cover the trainee's living expenses. The trainee typically is expected to cover all international and domestic travel costs to and from the training location, as well as personal expenses. As a general rule, arrangements for permanent housing are difficult to make prior to the trainee's arrival. It is advisable to bring a sufficient amount of savings to support the first month of living expenses. The employer and cooperating organization may provide assistance with the location of housing; however, the trainee usually must assume the primary responsibility for locating and financing housing.

Requirements

You must be at least 18 years of age at the time of application, and not more than 35. You must have graduated with a degree for the profession in which you are seeking training. Significant experience in the field, as determined by AIPT and its counterparts, may be substituted in the absence of a degree.

Application Procedures

There is an application fee of $150. Write AIPT for an application.

Contact:

Association for International Practical Training
10 Corporate Center, Suite 250
10400 Little Patuxent Parkway
Columbia, MD 21044-3510

THE ATLANTIC COUNCIL
OF THE UNITED STATES

The Atlantic Council of the United States was founded in 1961 as a non-profit center addressing the advancement of U.S. interests engaged in the issues now before the Atlantic and Pacific communities. The council's purpose is to identify challenges and opportunities, illuminate choices, and foster informed public debate about U.S., foreign, security and international economic policies, alone and in their interrelationships. The council works to engage the American government, corporate, professional and educational communities in an integrated program of policy studies and roundtable discussions, briefings, dialogues, conferences and publications, designed to support its selected membership and other constituencies as they reflect and plan for the future.

The Atlantic Council offers internships for undergraduate and graduate students with a variety of interests, including international security and defense issues, NATO, international economics and corporate affairs, Atlantic-Pacific relations, East-West relations, international education, energy policy and the environment, arms control/non-proliferation, civil-military relations and Eastern European/USSR transition. Interns also are invited to attend the council's programs, roundtables and other events.

The Atlantic Council is organized into three major program areas: West-West and NATO Programs; East-West Programs; and Atlantic-Pacific Programs. The Offices of Education, Development and Public Affairs, as well as the Office of Programs and Projects, all engage in activities dealing in all three of the program areas. Internships are available with all of the above offices. You are asked to indicate your fields of interest at the time of application.

Interns at the Atlantic Council support the various international public affairs and education programs. Interns generally spend the majority of their hours in this support activity. Their remaining time is spent attending Atlantic Council project discussions, conferences at other Washington-area policy study groups, and pursuing personal research interests connected with their studies.

In addition, the Atlantic Council sponsors an Intern Discussion Series (IDS) for its interns in the fall, spring and summer. The IDS program is a weekly roundtable discussion on current issues with Atlantic Council program directors and prominent individuals from the Washington area. IDS is designed to offer its interns the opportunity to engage in substantive discussion with public and foreign policy experts.

Internships are offered on a voluntary basis, and transportation and housing are strictly the responsibility of the intern. Academic credit may be obtained through your university or college.

Requirements

Atlantic Council internships are not research-oriented; rather, most of the work involves the development, planning and execution of various programs and projects. Interns must be able to type and prepare correspondence, use a computer system and word-processing equipment, be capable of self-guided research, organize meetings, have excellent communications skills, and be able to take on projects and carry them to fruition.

Application Procedures

A complete application consists of a cover letter, resume, academic transcripts (copies are acceptable), brief writing sample, transcript and two letters of recommendation (either professional or academic). These materials should be submitted to the council's intern coordinator at least eight weeks prior to an anticipated starting date (although applications are considered on a rolling basis). Interns are considered for positions throughout the year and are asked to commit a minimum of 10 to 12 weeks to the program.

Contact:

Intern Coordinator
The Atlantic Council of the United States
1616 H Street, N.W.
Washington, D.C. 20006
telephone (202)347-9353

Bei Jing–Washington, Inc.

Beijing-Washington, Inc., is the exclusive representative to China for over 30 American and European firms that manufacture electronic production-line equipment. Since 1979, Beijing-Washington, Inc., has sold this production equipment to leading manufacturers in China's electronics industry.

Beijing-Washington, Inc., offers internships at its Washington, D.C., area headquarters (located in the Maryland suburbs). Applicants may apply for spring, fall or summer. Duties are largely administrative at first, involving typing, word processing, filing and copying. Interns assist project managers with mailing, writing Chinese addresses, responding to requests from buyers and/or factories in China, and assisting with research projects.

The internships are approximately 16 hours per week. There is no salary offered, but there is a possibility of the internship developing into a full-time paid position.

Requirements

Candidates need not have the ability to write and speak Mandarin, but language proficiency is a plus. They must have an active interest in developing business in and with China.

Application Procedures

Send a resume along with dates you are available to Beijing-Washington, Inc.

Contact:

Beijing-Washington, Inc.
4340 East West Highway
Suite 200
Bethesda, MD 20814
telephone (301)656-4801

Bermuda Biological Station for Research, Inc.

The Bermuda Biological Station for Research (BBSR) is an independent research facility located on the island of Bermuda in the Atlantic Ocean. Incorporated in 1926, BBSR maintains 20 well-equipped laboratories, an oceanographic vessel and an array of sophisticated equipment for biological and chemical work conducted by the facility staff and visiting scientists and students. In addition to programs that offer financial support to help defray on-site research costs for faculty and students, BBSR offers a work-study program and a graduate internship program.

The Work-Study, or Volunteer, Program provides beginning students with opportunities to gain experience as research assistants.

Students who receive room and board at the station are obligated to work from 9 a.m. to noon and from 1 p.m. to 5 p.m. on weekdays and some weekends. Non-resident students may arrange individual schedules with their supervisors. Students spend approximately half the work week on assigned maintenance duties (clerical work and facility care and cleaning) and half on laboratory work under the supervision of a scientist. Lengths of stay can be from four weeks to four months.

Graduate students can apply for Visiting Internship Awards. Interns receive free housing and use of laboratory facilities for thesis research in exchange for performing teaching assistant duties ten hours per week. Duties usually include leading field trips, lecturing to visiting groups and preparing educational materials. Intern appointments last from six to 12 months, with possible renewal for a second year.

Requirements

Students applying for the Work-Study Program must be at least 18 years old and able to demonstrate maturity, independence and an interest and aptitude in the sciences. A $50 deposit is required of resident students to be held against telephone bills, room damage and key loss.

Students applying for Visiting Internship Awards must be M.S. or Ph.D. candidates in marine biology, marine chemistry, carbonate geology or oceanography.

Application Procedures

For the Work-Study Program, write to BBSR requesting an application form. You'll be asked to return the completed form with your resume to the work-study coordinator. For Visiting Internship Awards, send a letter of interest, a concise research proposal, graduate transcripts and two letters of recommendation to the Assistant Director for Education.

Contact:

Bermuda Biological Station for Research, Inc.
Ms. Nan Godet, Work-Study Coordinator or
Dr. Susan Cook, Assistant Director for Education
17 Biological Lane
Ferry Reach GE 01
Bermuda
telephone (809)297-1880

The Brookings Institution

The Brookings Institution in Washington, D.C., is a private, non-partisan organization that serves as an independent analyst on the workings of the U.S. government. The organization's research concentrates on political institutions, policy-making and policy issues.

Brookings offers a governmental studies program in which interns provide research assistance for current projects. Interns might be working in the areas of federalism, fair-trade laws, social policy, the future of political parties, Congress and the media, or the courts and Congress. Interns are encouraged to take advantage of presentations and discussions held at Brookings. The positions are unpaid and usually are for one semester. Students are accepted year-round for full- or part-time positions.

Requirements

Applicants should be college juniors, seniors or graduate students. They should have a background in American government and political science. It is important to have an eye for details. Research and library skills are not required, but are desirable.

Application Procedures

Send a resume, two letters of recommendation, a writing sample and a transcript with course descriptions of all political science credits. All application materials should be received one month before the desired starting time.

Contact:

The Brookings Institution
Governmental Studies Program
Sue Thompson, Program Assistant
1775 Massachusetts Avenue, NW
Washington, D.C. 20036
telephone (202)797-6052

The Brother's Brother Foundation

The Brother's Brother Foundation (BBF) sends U.S. surplus and donated goods to approximately 40 developing countries and island groups. The vast majority of goods shipped tend to be textbooks and medical supplies. Shipments during 1988 totalled $36 million. While BBF does not assign personnel to work overseas, trustees and staff make occasional visits to check on distribution of goods shipped.

BBF hires interns to work in its Pittsburgh office for a salary or hourly wages. The duration of an internship can be as long as two years, though shorter periods are more common.

Requirements

Almost all of BBF's interns are drawn from the University of Pittsburgh's Graduate School of Public Affairs. Interns usually are part-way through their master's program and are residents of Pittsburgh. Compensation is seldom adequate for those who do not live in the Pittsburgh area already.

Application Procedures

Send a letter of application and resume.

Contact:

Brother's Brother Foundation
Mr. Luke Hingson, Executive Director
824 Grandview Avenue
Pittsburgh, PA 15211
telephone (412)431-1600

CARE is a non-profit, non-sectarian, independent relief and development organization. Its purpose is to help the developing world's poor in their efforts to achieve social and economic well-being. CARE offers technical assistance, training, food, other material resources and management in combinations appropriate to local needs and priorities.

CARE has no overseas volunteer positions—it hires a limited number of international staff employees—but it does accept volunteers to work in its domestic field offices.

Requirements

There are no specific requirements for volunteers.

Application Procedures

Write to CARE for an application questionnaire. The application will ask you about your special interests and abilities, etc.

Contact:

CARE
660 First Avenue
New York, NY 10016
telephone (212)686-3110

CARIBBEAN
CONSERVATION
C O R P O R A T I O N

The Caribbean Conservation Corporation (CCC) administers the longest ongoing turtle-tagging project in the world at its field station in Tortuguero, Costa Rica. It offers about six two-month research assistantships from July 1 through September 15. Research assistants help CCC scientists tag nesting turtles and perform beach surveys. The majority of the work is done on the beach at night, although there are some daytime activities. Taggers usually work in shifts of four hours a night (8 p.m. to midnight or midnight to 4 a.m.), six days per week. The work is physically demanding and occasionally exhausting. There also are opportunities to help with other CCC activities, including computerization of data, coordination of volunteers and environmental education.

Internships can be arranged and are encouraged through existing university programs. The CCC will coordinate field activities if the student selects an academic adviser at his/her institution. Credit must be arranged through the student's college or university. The Tortuguero field station provides unlimited opportunity for research on sea turtles, tropical fresh-water ecology, lowland rain-forest flora and fauna and related subjects. Students with internships are encouraged to design an independent project.

July through September is the nesting season of the endangered green turtle. Research assistants are expected to arrive in Tortuguero one week before the season begins for training. Although early arrival is required, departure dates are flexible.

Research assistants/interns are responsible for covering all costs of transportation to and from Tortuguero, Costa Rica. Food and lodging are provided by CCC. Stipends are available.

Requirements

You must be at least 20 years of age, hard-working and be able to demonstrate responsibility and self-motivation, as well as a keen interest in wildlife and resource conservation. In addition, you must have an educational background in biological or marine sciences, wildlife management, resource conservation, environmental education or related fields. Current students or recent graduates are preferred.

Conversational Spanish is required, as assistants work closely with Costa Rican counterparts.

Application Procedures

You must complete an application form and submit it to the Director of Programs by February 28. You must include: a cover letter expressing your desire to participate in the program and detailing your personal strengths and interests; a resume or curriculum vitae; a statement of your level of proficiency in the Spanish language; and the names, addresses and telephone numbers of three professional or academic references.

Contact:

Director of Programs
RA/Internship Program
Caribbean Conservation Corp.
P.O. Box 2866
Gainesville, FL 32602

CDS International, Inc., is a private, non-profit organization established in 1968 to promote the interests of international business through international professional training. It administers exchange programs between Germany and the United States, two for Americans and one for Germans.

Congress-Bundestag Program
CDS International, Inc.

CDS Career Training Program

The Career Training Program offers young professionals an opportunity to learn German and work at a paid position for a German company for a period of one year to 18 months. Language training takes up the first one to three months of the period, with intensive study at the Carl Duisberg Center in Cologne or Munich. During this time the participant boards with a local German family.

Requirements

Applicants for the Career Training Program should have a college degree in a business, engineering or technical field, or training in the hotel industry or as a bilingual secretary; a good knowledge of German; and one to two years of full-time work experience.

CDS Internship Program

The CDS Internship Program offers language training, usually for one month at the Carl Duisberg Center, followed by a paid internship for approximately six months. Program participants are required to pay some of the program costs in most cases. Costs are dependent upon the amount of formal language training required, the prevailing exchange rates and time of year. Costs are estimated at $1,500, excluding airfare. A limited number of stipends and other financial assistance are available.

Requirements

Applicants for the Internship Program should be enrolled currently in, or a recent graduate of, an accredited university with a major in a business, technical or agricultural field. They should have a good knowledge of German.

Congress-Bundestag Program

The Congress-Bundestag Program is a year-long, work-study exchange program designed to strengthen ties between the younger generations of Germany and the United States. It was conceived and is supported by members of the U.S. Congress and the German Bundestag, and is supported financially by the U.S. Information Agency. This program includes two months of language study, classroom instruction at a German technical school or other institution of higher education for about four months, then placement in an internship with a German company for about six months. This program also includes a pre-departure orientation seminar in Washington, D.C., living accommodations with either a German host family or in a dormitory, seminars in Berlin at mid-year and in Bonn at the end of the year, and a final evaluation seminar in New York.

Requirements

The Congress-Bundestag Program is a competitive scholarship program for 18- to 24-year-old young professionals. You must be a high-school graduate with a good record of academic achievement and have a well-defined career goal, with full- or part-time work experience related to your prospective career.

Application Procedures

Write to CDS to receive application forms and program information. Applicants for the Career Training Program should return completed applications four months before the anticipated departure date. Those for the internship program should return their applications five months before one of the starting dates, which are in January, March, April, September and October. Applications for the Congress-Bundestag Program must be submitted by mid-January.

Contact for All Programs:

CDS International, Inc.
330 Seventh Ave.
New York, NY 10001
telephone (212)760-1400

CENTRAL BUREAU

The Central Bureau for Educational Visits and Exchanges, a British organization, in cooperation with the Association for International Practical Training (AIPT) in the United States, administers the U.S./U.K. Career Development Program. This program assists in arranging practical training in the United Kingdom for Americans, and in the United States for U.K. citizens. The program was developed with the approval of the British Home Office and the U.S. and British embassies, to promote transnational training for qualified individuals. The objective of the program is to enable participants to gain practical work experience for a maximum of 18 months in the United States or Britain. Jobs offered to trainees provide professional training of a kind that will develop a participant's capabilities in his or her chosen field.

The application procedure takes approximately six to eight weeks. After a trainee's application has been approved by the Central Bureau and AIPT, the employer is expected to complete an offer-of-training form. The Central Bureau then issues a Certificate of Appointment, which stands in lieu of a work permit. This certificate allows the trainee to work in the United Kingdom for a maximum of 18 months. If the trainee already is in the United Kingdom, then he/she will have to return to the United States for approximately three weeks to obtain the necessary migration papers.

There is an application fee of $150 payable to AIPT on submission of the application form, and a processing fee of 450 British pounds payable to the Central Bureau. The latter is paid by either the British employer or the trainee upon approval of the application. The British Embassy in Washington also levies a fee of $150 for the processing of paper work. When applicants arrive in the United Kingdom they must register with the police. This costs about 40 British pounds. Once in the United Kingdom, trainees must pay U.K. income taxes. They also will be liable for local poll tax or Community Charge. Applicants must pay for Britain's National Insurance, which entitles them to medical coverage under the National Health Service.

Requirements

Participants must be aged between 19 and 35. They must find their own work placement in the United Kingdom. They must have had at least one to two years' work experience and/or qualifications in their chosen field. They must not change jobs without good reason and full consultation with the Central Bureau.

Application Procedures

Write the Central Bureau for an application form.

Contact:

U.S./U.K. Career Development Programme
Vocational and Technical Education Department
Central Bureau for Educational Visits and Exchanges
Seymour Mews House
Seymour Mews
London W1H 9PE
England

The Chol-Chol Foundation for Human Development is a non-profit corporation for the elimination of hunger through self-help. It provides technical assistance and arranges loans to farmers in Chile and Nigeria.

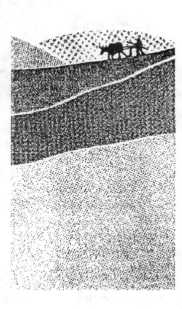

The foundation uses interns at the Washington, D.C., office. The positions are unpaid and may be full- or part-time. The length of the internship is flexible. Interns are involved in proposal preparation, correspondence, research, and work with government agencies concerned with Third World development.

Requirements

Applicants should be college students with an interest in international development.

Application Procedures

Send a letter with relevant background and career-goal information to the director of Chol-Chol Foundation. Interviews are requested of all applicants.

Contact:

Chol-Chol Foundation
V.W. Mondell, Executive Director
3421 M Street, NW
Suite 1343
Washington, D.C. 20007
telephone (703)525-8844

Communicating for Agriculture (CA) is a national, non-profit association of people working in all aspects of agriculture and agribusiness, which offers the Communicating for Agriculture Exchange Program (CAEP). The goals of the exchange program are to provide agricultural experience, promote cultural understanding and encourage the study of a foreign language. Programs have been held in Australia, Brazil, Canada, Denmark, Holland, Norway, Sweden, France, West Germany, Ireland, Switzerland and New Zealand.

Participants live and work with a host family or business. There are five program options from which to choose: the agricultural program; the horticultural program; the agri-home program; the agri-mix program, which is a combination of the first three programs; and the agribusiness program. Some typical examples of placements are with dairy farms, horticultural businesses, sheep farms, veterinarians or with seed companies. The European programs can last from three to 13 months and the other programs from six to 13 months. Trainees receive room, board and a stipend from the host family. The approximate cost for the program is $1,500 to $4,200, depending upon the country and the length of the stay. Covered expenses are round-trip airfare, insurance, administrative costs and transportation to the host family. The fee does not include transportation costs to the U.S. departure point or the travel costs when going from the host family to the foreign departure point.

Requirements

Applicants should be 18 to 28 years of age, healthy, single and have a valid drivers license. At least one year of experience in your field of interest is required. The desire to live and work in a different culture is important. The CAEP encourages trainees to learn something about the language of the host country before they go and to continue to study while in the program.

Application Procedures

Return the completed application with eight passport photos, two references and an autobiography. A deposit of $300 is due with the application and, if you are not placed, $225 will be refunded. The applications are due three months before departure. Those interested in the agribusiness program should allow four months. Departures for Europe are in April and June. For the Australia, New Zealand and Brazil programs, departures are in April and September or October.

Contact:

Communicating for Agriculture
Marty Gibson, Coordinator
2626 E. 82nd Street
Suite 325
Bloomington, MN 55425
telephone (800)445-1525 or (612)854-9005

Cooperative Housing Foundation

The Cooperative Housing Foundation (CHF) was established in 1952. Its early work was primarily in the United States, but since 1962, it has provided housing-related assistance to 80 developing countries.

This organization employs interns in its Silver Spring, Maryland, office. Internships vary in duration and can be arranged for areas such as computer work, library work, research, fund raising and audio-visual work. Positions are salaried. This is an informal program offering a variety of internship opportunities.

Requirements

Appropriate college work is needed, depending on the job the intern is to be doing. CHF seeks people who are concerned about issues of low-income housing both at home and abroad.

Application Procedures

A resume can be sent at any time during the year to the intern coordinator. An application will be sent to you to be completed and returned with a one- to two-page writing sample.

Contact:

Cooperative Housing Foundation (CHF)
Mr. James Trousdale, Intern Coordinator
1010 Wayne Avenue
Silver Spring, MD 20910
telephone (301)587-4700
fax (301)587-2626

Council on Hemispheric Affairs

The Council on Hemispheric Affairs (COHA) was founded in 1975 as a non-profit, independent research organization. Its main focus is to promote the common interests of the hemisphere. It monitors and encourages constructive U.S. policies toward Latin America and promotes good relations between Canada and Latin America.

COHA's internship program has been in existence since 1976 and has had over 800 interns at its Washington, D.C., location. Competition is keen for these positions, which are voluntary. They are from 9:00 a.m. to 5:30 p.m. every work day and last from 13 to 16 weeks (13 weeks for summer interns).

Interns are involved in all aspects of COHA's work. They write for its biweekly publication, conduct research, conduct interviews with policy-makers, and provide information to the general public, journalists, etc. Generally two-thirds of the interns' time is spent on writing or research activities and one-third on administrative tasks. Professional staff vacancies always are filled by former interns.

Requirements

Candidates should be highly motivated and have an interest or background in U.S./Latin American affairs or international affairs. Some knowledge of Spanish or Portuguese is desirable. Strong research and writing skills are essential.

Application Procedures

Send a resume, transcript with relevant courses taken, and a writing sample.

Contact:

Secretary of Internships
Council on Hemispheric Affairs
724 9th Street, NW, Suite 401
Washington, D.C. 20009
telephone (202)393-3322
fax (202)393-3423

Development Associates, Inc. (DAI), is an international consulting firm that concentrates on two major development areas: agriculture and natural resources; and finance, management and economics. It has worked in 80 countries since its founding in 1970. DAI is  among the prominent suppliers of technical assistance to organizations like the U.S. Agency for International Development, the World Bank and the U.N. Development Programme.

DAI's internships are very informal and are offered in a wide variety of projects. Interns are unpaid and work in the Arlington, Virginia, office. Summer or winter internships are possible.

Requirements

Candidates must have good writing skills. Other qualifications may be required, depending upon the project.

Application Procedures

Send a resume and a cover letter specifying your interest.

Contact:

Development Associates, Inc.
1730 North Lynn Street
Arlington, VA 22209-2004
telephone (703)276-0677

Elwyn (EI) offers rehabilitation services for the mentally and physically disabled. It has a number of offices around the United States and one in Israel. The Israel office in Jerusalem offers programs in adult training, vocational training, mental health services, diagnostic evaluations, a rehabilitation kindergarten, residential services, a child development center, medical and dental services, work-study, ancillary support services, recreation and leisure, educational services, supported employment and a pre-vocational program for autistic young adults.

Elwyn does not have a regular internship program, but it does sponsor practicum experiences in psychology, education, rehabilitation and social work. These generally are unpaid, vary in duration according to need, and are limited to persons in accredited degree programs in the fields mentioned.

Requirements

You must be in an accredited degree program in psychology, education, rehabilitation or social work.

Application Procedures

Send a letter with the details of your interest in a practicum experience.

Contact:

Elwyn
Elwyn, PA 19063
telephone (215)891-2000

ÉMIGRÉ MEMORIAL
GERMAN INTERNSHIP PROGRAMS

Émigré Memorial German Internship Programs (EMGIP) are work-study opportunities for advanced undergraduate and graduate students interested in German affairs.

The organization places about 14 interns per year. The programs are conducted by scholars on an independent, voluntary basis, in cooperation with the offices concerned. Founded and coordinated by Professor George Romoser, EMGIP solicits nominations from members of the Conference Group on German Politics, an independent organization founded in 1968, as well as from other groups active in German affairs; however, applications are open to all qualified persons. An independent selection committee of scholars and former interns choose the current interns.

EMGIP is not otherwise affiliated with any particular college, university or organization. These internships neither require tuition nor provide for college or university course credits. They have no resemblance to semester-abroad or similar intern programs in the Bundestag.

Following are the three internship programs:

Informationszentrum Berlin

In this program, interns receive a general overview of political life and government in Berlin. The internship involves interviews and meetings with a wide variety of Berlin officials and visitors to Berlin, translating, working on brochures, and aiding visiting groups. This internship is especially suited for seniors and beginning graduate students. The stipend is 1200 Deutchemarks per month.

Deutscher Bundestag, Bonn

This internship involves work-study in the administrative, legislative research, and political (deputies, committees) areas of the German Parliament, including ample contact with legislative experts. Applicants should be familiar with Bundestag structure. When applying, they must indicate preference for two areas of interest and for affiliation with a particular Bundestag fraction. This program especially is suited for graduate students who are at intermediate and advanced stages of their degree work. The stipend is 2000 Deutchemarks per month.

Hessicher and Thuringer Landtage

This program is a one-month internship to observe the workings of a German state parliament. No undergraduates are accepted. There is no stipend.

Requirements

Candidates may come from any non-German-speaking country (the emphasis is on selection from North America), and must possess sufficient fluency in German at the time of application to perform assigned functions competently, and engage in discussions at all levels of German society. An oral examination is given prior to nomination, during the final selection process.

Generally, candidates must have some background in the social sciences or humanities related to the social sciences; a degree in German language/literature normally is not sufficient for these programs.

Application Procedures

Contact EMGIP for an information brochure. Your application should include five copies of answers to 13 questions in the brochure. The questions include information on your education and call for a written essay on why you are interested in EMGIP's programs. Your application also should include five copies of transcripts for each college/university attended; three letters of recommendation; a recent photo; and a non-refundable processing fee to support administrative costs. The processing fee is $85 if applying to all programs; $60 if applying only to the Bundestag Program; and $45 if applying only to the Berlin and/or Landtage Programs.

EMGIP cautions applicants that they should not send materials via express mail, special delivery, or commercial courier, etc., as this will only delay acceptance and processing of your application. Send your application only by regular or air mail.

EMGIP also requests that applicants not telephone them.

Contact for All Programs:

German Internships (EMGIP)
P.O. Box 345
Durham, NH 03824

GLOBAL 🌐 EXCHANGE

Global Exchange is a non-profit research, education and action center that was formed in 1988 to help advance the internationalist citizen movement. It seeks to build more people-to-people ties between the United States and the Third World and closer collaboration between U.S. groups doing such work. Programs include material assistance campaigns; reality tours to Third World countries; development of educational resources, including writing articles, publishing books and guides to work in the Third World; as well as coordinating speaking tours and forums on important issues.

Global Exchange accepts interns in its San Francisco office to help in organizing tours, raising funds, alternative trade, its partnership program, its publications, research, and organizing special events. No stipends are available, but Global Exchange may be able to find inexpensive housing.

Requirements

Applicants must be self-motivated, creative and willing to make a set time commitment, depending on the project.

Application Procedures

Send a query letter and a resume.

Contact:

Global Exchange
2141 Mission Street Room 202
San Francisco, CA 94110
telephone (415)255-7296
fax (415)255-7498

GRASSROOTS INTERNATIONAL

Grassroots International is an independent development and information agency. It channels humanitarian aid to democratic social-change movements in the Third World and informs the U.S. public about Third World conflicts and crises.

Grassroots International offers several internships in its Cambridge office. Interns assist in project administration and information processing for overseas programs in the Middle East, Africa and the Philippines. Interns' tasks include coordinating the flow of information in and out of the agency; corresponding with overseas partners and maintaining current project files; maintaining contacts with local and national organizations working on similar issues; mail processing; and filling information requests.

Interns are unpaid and work 15 to 20 hours per week.

Requirements

Applicants must have initiative, organizational skills, writing ability, computer aptitude and a strong interest in Third World issues.

Application Procedures

Submit a letter of interest and a resume.

Contact:

Catherine Brady
Grassroots International
P.O. Box 312
Cambridge, MA 02139
telephone (617)497-9180
fax (617)497-4397

The Heritage Foundation

The Heritage Foundation was established in 1973 as an independent public policy research and education organization. Its programs aim to give responsible conservatism a voice in U.S. and world affairs. The foundation is involved in research, publishing and lectures, and holds debates on domestic and economic policy, foreign policy and defense, and Asian Studies.

Interns at the Heritage Foundation do various research and clerical jobs under the direction of department heads. The 15 to 20 interns are urged to take advantage of various educational programs and conferences sponsored by the Heritage Foundation. Summer interns work 9:00 a.m. to 5:30 p.m. every work day for about 12 weeks, and receive about $200 per week. There also are opportunities for unpaid positions during the academic year that offer a flexible work schedule.

Requirements

Applicants for internships should be college students with an interest in public policy, and have a conservative outlook on policy issues.

Application Procedures

Send a resume, a cover letter stating why you want to be an intern, references or letters of recommendation, and any other pertinent materials, such as writing samples. These materials should be received between January 1 and March 15. All applicants will receive notification by the end of April.

Contact:

The Heritage Foundation
Mr. Robert Huberty, Director
Academic Programs
214 Massachusetts Ave., N.E.
Washington, D.C. 20002
telephone (202)546-4400

The Institute of International Education (IIE), located in Mexico City, hosts an intern program for college students who wish to gain experience in an overseas educational counseling center. IIE functions as an integral part of the U.S. Information Service in Mexico, providing information about U.S. education to more than 35,000 people per year. IIE maintains close ties with the American Embassy, Mexican government offices, and universities and colleges both in Mexico and the United States.

Interns at the IIE office in Mexico have the opportunity to work as student advisers, giving out information about U.S. educational opportunities. They also have the chance to observe and familiarize themselves with the operations of a large U.S. embassy. Office duties include advising the public about all aspects of U.S. education; providing information about admissions and special American testing programs such as SAT and GRE; working on special research projects assigned by the director or assistant director; and assisting with special programs such as pre-departure orientation, seminars for visiting professors, etc. Interns are allowed one free day per week to take advantage of cultural activities.

Internships usually are for two months, but can be extended in special circumstances. IIE tries to help interns with housing and travel when possible. Interns receive $500 for a two-month internship.

Requirements

Applicants must have completed at least two years of college in the United States and must be able to communicate well in both Spanish and English. They must make a specific time commitment of a summer or term and must have the personal finances to cover travel, lodging, meals and personal expenses. They must have a general knowledge of Mexican history and culture and are expected to keep abreast of current political, economic, educational and social events in Mexico. Interns must possess personal maturity, as demonstrated by the ability to receive instruction, and work on projects with limited supervision. They must have the ability to adapt to, and benefit from, new cultural experiences.

Application Procedures

You should obtain an application form and return it to IIE with a copy of your university transcript and two letters of recommendation (one from someone who can attest to your ability in Spanish). This is a competitive program; therefore, applications should be made approximately three months in advance.

Contact:

IIE
Educational Counseling Center
P.O. Box 3087
Laredo, TX 78044
telephone 011 (525)211-0042, ext. 3500

The Instituto Guatemalteco Americano (IGA) is a center for cultural exchange between Guatemala and the United States. It is located in Guatemala City and offers a library, videos on American life, English courses, various cultural exhibits and performances, and other programs and information.

IGA has offered internships in cultural activities, the library, the English department, the bilingual secretarial department and the educational advising center. Interns work on special-interest projects related to Guatemala or

Instituto Guatemalteco Americano

to the department sponsoring the internship. The internships are from four to eight weeks in the summer. All expenses for transportation, room, board and personal expenses are the responsibility of the intern. IGA helps interns in making housing and travel arrangements.

Requirements

Applicants must have completed at least two years of college and be able to communicate in Spanish. Interns working in the English department may not need the Spanish requirement. Specific internships may have other requirements. IGA recommends the program for those who have majored in Latin American studies, Spanish or education, but the program also is open to those in other fields. Maturity and adaptability are necessary qualities for applicants. It is important for interns to have some knowledge of Guatemala before they arrive and they are expected to keep up with current events during their stay. IGA also expects interns to take advantage of the various cultural and educational opportunities that are offered at the center.

Application Procedures

IGA has specific information on available internships and can send you an application. The completed applications, two letters of recommendation and an official transcript are due two months before the start of the internship. One of the recommendations should come from a Spanish professor, except in the case of those applying for internships in the English department.

Contact:

Educational Advisor
ACAO/BNCD
USEMB/USIS
Unit 3318
APO AA 34024

INTERNATIONAL ASSOCIATION FOR THE EXCHANGE OF STUDENTS FOR TECHNICAL EXPERIENCE UNITED STATES

The International Association for the Exchange of Students for Technical Experience (IASTE) is an organization with a membership of over 50 countries. The program's goal is to provide a unique combination of on-the-job practical training and the experience of living in another culture. IAESTE aims to promote technological progress and facilitate an understanding between different peoples and cultures. Since 1950, IAESTE has placed American students in internships with employers worldwide.

Full-time, on-the-job training is provided for students in engineering, computer science, architecture, natural and physical sciences, mathematics and agriculture. Positions are available in industry, research institutes, universities, consulting firms, laboratories and other organizations. Approximately 60 percent of IAESTE traineeships are in engineering and 20 percent are in computer sciences.

Although training periods can last as long as 18 months, the majority of the positions last eight to 13 weeks during the summer months, the time when most full-time students are available to participate. It is possible to commence training during the fall, but there are not as many opportunities at this time of year.

IAESTE successfully places only 40 percent of its American applicants each year. Because the IAESTE program is reciprocal, you can increase your chance of placement by finding an American employer who is interested in hiring a foreign trainee through IAESTE. While finding such an employer is not a requirement of IAESTE, doing so will give you first consideration for positions available within your field of study.

An allowance is paid by the employer adequate to cover living expenses during the traineeship. You must pay a $75 application fee, international transportation to and from your place of employment, for recreational and other incidental expenses, and for insurance coverage (you must be covered before departure).

Requirements

You must be enrolled as a full-time university student at the time the application is received, and you must be studying in a technical field. Eligible foreign students studying in the United States may apply; however, IAESTE international agreements prevent placement in either the United States or the home countries of these students.

Application Procedures

The application deadline for summer placements is December 10. Reciprocal offers from U.S. employers must be submitted to AIPT by January 10.

Contact:

> IAESTE
> 10400 Little Patuxent Parkway, Suite 250
> Columbia, MD 21044-3510
> telephone (410)997-2200

The International Association of Students in Economics and Business Management (referred to by its French acronym, AIESEC) is a student managed business association whose goal is to promote international peace through understanding. One of the ways AIESEC accomplishes its goal is through an international internship program. AIESEC offers students the practical business experience needed in order to become effective global managers.

AIESEC is open to all interested students, either graduate or undergraduate, regardless of major. The actual exchange process works on a reciprocal basis. Each local committee raises a job for a student from abroad and earns a credit to send one of its members on an international traineeship. The traineeship takes place in one of the 69 countries with AIESEC committees and is determined by the specific work interests of the student. Each local committee has its own guidelines for obtaining credits for internships.

Internships may last from six weeks to 18 months. The fee to join AIESEC is from $25 to $50, depending on the chapter. The internships are paid—the amount is enough for room and board. Interns must pay for their own transportation and insurance. There is a placement fee of $150.

Requirements

In order to participate in the AIESEC exchange, students must join AIESEC at their university. The longer students are with AIESEC, the more they will develop as global business leaders, and the better their chances will be to receive a credit to participate in the AIESEC exchange program. People should not join AIESEC just before graduation in the hope of attaining a job abroad. If there is not an AIESEC chapter at your university you may write to the address below for information.

Application Procedures

Contact your local college or university chapter for information on joining AIESEC. If your school does not have an AIESEC chapter, write AIESEC directly.

Contact:

AIESEC-United States
National Office
841 Broadway
Suite 608
New York, NY 10003
telephone (212)757-3774

International Business-Government Counsellors, Inc. (IBC), was one of the first international government-relations firms in the United States. The organization analyzes how the policies of the United States and other governments affect the international economy. It does research for international corporations and helps them develop strategies to respond to government policies.

IBC interns usually monitor and report on Capitol Hill hearings that concern international trade and do research at the Department of Commerce or other agencies. Internships are offered in the spring, summer and winter. They generally last a semester or, during the summer, 10 to 12 weeks. They may be part- or full-time, but all are unpaid positions. It may be possible to earn academic credit through your university by working as an intern with IBC.

Requirements

The IBC is looking for college students who are able to work with minimum supervision.

Application Procedures

There is no specific deadline for application. Send a resume, college transcript and writing sample.

Contact:

International Business-Government Counsellors, Inc.
Guy L. Escolme
818 Connecticut Ave., NW, 12th Floor
Washington, D.C. 20006
telephone (202)872-8181
fax (202)876-8696

IVS INTERNATIONAL VOLUNTARY SERVICES, INC.

International Voluntary Services, Inc. (IVS), is a private, international development agency. IVS recruits volunteers to serve around the world, providing technical assistance to fight against hunger, poverty, and inequality in Asia, Latin America and southern Africa. It also recruits interns for its Washington, D.C., office.

IVS uses interns on an as-needed basis. Interns generally work with a regional program coordinator for Africa, Asia or Latin America. They attend program meetings, staff meetings and review sessions, as their schedules permit. They carry out research, support the program staff or work on other projects as needed. The work is for approximately eight hours per week, for a semester or one year. The positions are unpaid.

Requirements

Applicants should be undergraduate college students who are interested in international development, especially in Asia, Africa or Latin America. They should have excellent writing and research skills.

Knowledge of WordPerfect and Lotus are a plus. Spanish is helpful for Latin America interns.

Application Procedures

Send a letter and a resume indicating your geographical area of interest.

Contact:

International Voluntary Services, Inc.
Recruitment Officer
1424 16th St. NW, Suite 204
Washington, D.C. 20036
telephone (202)387-5533
fax (202)387-4234

For information on IVIS volunteer opportunities, see the section later in this book titled "International Volunteer Opportunities with Private Organizations."

Interns for Peace (IFP) is a program begun in 1977, to improve relations and understanding between the Jews and Arabs in Israel. Interns are trained and placed in teams in Arab and Jewish communities to develop needed projects that fit the interns' skills. Projects range from  regional art, music, or theater festivals, to a group formed to discuss issues of concern for Israeli Jewish and Israeli Arab women. Projects are selected specifically to promote Jewish-Arab cooperation.

An intensive one-month study period begins the two-year commitment. Interns take courses in such areas as Jewish-Arab relations, Israeli society, community work and conflict resolution. During the training period, visits are made to the communities where the program operates. As they work in the communities, interns continue to receive training in Arabic, group dynamics or other helpful areas.

The communities provide housing to the interns and they receive a stipend of approximately $500 a month. Medical coverage and insurance are provided. The typical intern works five and a half days per week and generally receives vacation during the month of August.

Requirements

Candidates must be Jews or Arabs from anywhere in the world. All must have a commitment to improving Jewish-Arab relations. A bachelor's, or equivalent degree, is required. At least an intermediate proficiency in Hebrew or Arabic is preferred. Prospective interns must have done previous community work and have spent at least six months in Israel. They may be single or married couples with or without children. Skills should be in one or more of the following areas: teaching, health care, youth work, sports, the arts, community organizing or business. Professional job experience is preferred. Other important attributes are the ability to work with those from a different culture, the ability to work in a team, creativity and flexibility.

Application Procedures

IFP requires completion of a biographical information form and three reference forms that are available from their office. Also required are a resume emphasizing relevant experience, two black-and-white glossy photos, and a essay of about 500 words on why you want to be part of the program. The essay should discuss why you are interested in working on Israeli-Arab relations through community work and why you wish to work for IFP instead of another organization also working to improve relations.

Applicants considered for the program will be interviewed by members of the Advisory Committee and a psychologist.

Contact:

Interns For Peace
270 West 89th St.
New York, NY 10024
telephone (212)580-0540
fax (212)580-0693

The Koc School, near Istanbul, Turkey, is a bilingual and bicultural, coeducational, secondary boarding school for Turkish youth, with an international faculty. It provides internships for graduating or recently graduated American college students who wish to teach overseas for a year. Called "teaching fellows," participants in the program work under the direct supervision of full-time faculty members who determine

assignments and work load, monitor progress and generally act as the fellows' supervisors and mentors.

Teaching fellows are housed on campus in a town house apartment. Their meals are taken free of charge in the school's dining room. They receive round-trip transportation to and from the United States, as well as medical and insurance benefits, and a monthly stipend that enables them to live well and travel in Turkey and neighboring countries. At the conclusion of a fellow's internship year, the school assists him or her in finding further international school employment either at Koc or elsewhere.

Requirements

You must be enthusiastic, highly motivated and flexible, with a superior educational background. You must have an undergraduate or graduate major in English, ESL, math or science, as well as a teaching certificate.

Application Procedures

Send a letter of application and credentials directly to the school.

Contact:

Gerald Shields
Deputy Headmaster
The Koc School
P.O. Box 38
Pendik - Istanbul, Turkey
telephone (90)(1)304-1048
fax (90)(1)304-1026

Legacy International

Legacy International, a non-profit, non-governmental organization affiliated with the United Nations, creates opportunities to address controversial issues through cooperation. Legacy sponsors programs for adults on intercultural relations, and a unique summer leadership program for youths. Internships are available year-round in Legacy's Alexandria, Virginia, office, and during the summer months at the summer program site in rural Bedford, Virginia.

Legacy's summer program brings together over 150 young people between the ages of 14 and 18, and staff from varied races, religions and national origins to participate in training programs dedicated to community organization, environmental responsibility, leadership, global issues and cross-cultural relations. It is residential and positions are for nine weeks, mid-June to mid-August, six and a half days per week, with 24-hour, on-site responsibility. Room, board and health insurance are provided for practicum interns. A negotiable stipend is provided for professional-level staff in teaching and non-teaching positions. All staff receive a two-week training program in intercultural relations.

Teaching positions are in leadership training, environmental education, global education, conflict management, ropes course, studio arts, English as a foreign language and performing arts. Non-teaching positions include administrative and program assistants, special-programming coordinator, certified water-safety instructor and support services, such as bookkeeping, secretarial, maintenance and kitchen.

Requirements

College students and recent graduates generally qualify for positions in Legacy's Practicum in Intercultural Relations, a credit-earning, unpaid internship. Applicants with professional-level expertise, and some college students, qualify for stipend-paying positions. Non-smokers only need apply. Those interested in the Practicum in Intercultural Relations must pay a $15 application fee.

Application Procedures for All Programs

Those interested in administrative internships in the Alexandria office can send a resume and cover letter any time.

To apply for the summer program, write or call Legacy's Bedford office in early February for updated information and an application.

Contact for All Programs:

Legacy International
346 Commerce Street
Alexandria, VA 22314
telephone (703)549-3630
fax (703)549-0262

Legacy International
Leila Baz, Assistant Director, Summer Program
Rt 4, Box 265-WW
Bedford, VA 24523
telephone (703)297-5982
fax (703)297-1860

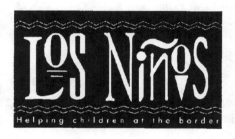

Established in 1974, Los Niños is dedicated to improving the quality of life for Mexican children and their families along the Mexican-U.S. border. It also is dedicated to providing education on the benefits of self-help community development through cultural interaction. The Los Niños Development Education Program annually provides hundreds of American interns with a unique educational experience. Interns work on projects located in Tijuana and Mexicali, Mexico. Los Niños offers three internship programs, described below.

Long-Term Internship Program

These internships last for a year or longer. Long-term interns work in Los Niños development projects in low-income communities. They assist Mexican coordinators in organizing educational community programs, such as nutrition or family gardening courses. They do research for the projects on which they work and network with organizations that share similar goals. They also attend weekly classes taught by a development expert.

Summer Internship Program

This program lasts for six weeks, beginning early July and ending mid-August. Interns from across the United States teach summer school in Tijuana communities and attend classes and cultural activities that teach them about Mexico and the border region. Full and partial scholarships are available.

Short-Term Education Program

Los Niños offers weekend and week-long programs from September through June. Groups of people study Tijuana and the border region in a short time frame. High-school, university, service and business groups interact with communities, hear local experts speak about the environment, human rights and economic issues in the border area, and visit cultural exhibits.

Requirements

Los Niños lists no specific requirements.

Application Procedures for All Programs

Write to Los Niños for an application, specifying the program in which you are interested.

Contact for All Programs:

Los Niños
9765 Marconi Drive, Suite 105
San Ysidro, CA 92173
telephone (619)661-6912

MAP–READER'S diqEST iNTERNATioNAL FellowsHips

The goal of the non-profit organization Medical Assistance Programs (MAP) International is to provide health care to the poor in nearly 80 developing countries. MAP takes donations of medical supplies, medicines, or cash and distributes them to needy areas of the world. The organization also aids in disaster relief.

MAP received a grant in 1971 from the founder of *Reader's Digest*, DeWitt Wallace. This grant established a program for medical students in their last year of medical school to learn about cultures and medical problems in developing nations. Another goal of the program is to encourage the students to be part of the Christian ministry administering health care to the Third World. Assignments generally are in outlying areas in a clinic, community health program or mission hospital. Students applying do not need to have the details for the internship already worked out, but they are encouraged to contact overseas missions and hospitals to find a position.

The grant pays for 75 percent of the most economical airfare. Students are responsible for the other 25 percent, plus other expenses, including room and board. Eight weeks is the minimum length of stay to qualify for the grant.

Requirements

Students usually are in their last year of a traditional medical school program or its equivalent. Some funds are available for those who have completed medical school and have not yet gone into private practice. Married students are encouraged to take their spouses, but no children under six months are allowed. Travel arrangements must be made through an agency designated by MAP. Grants are in effect for one year.

Application Procedures

Applications are considered by the selection committee twice a year. Applications should be received before December 1, to be considered at the March meeting, and before June 1, to be considered at the September meeting. All applications must be typed. Representatives of MAP will interview all applicants. The departure date should be at least three months after the selection committee meetings.

Contact:

MAP International
RDIF Coordinator
2200 Glynco Parkway
P.O. Box 50
Brunswick, GA 31521

The Middle East Institute

The Middle East Institute (MEI) is a non-profit organization that works to improve the public's knowledge and understanding of the Middle East. It uses lectures, courses, conferences and publications to meet this goal.

The Washington, D.C., office uses interns for the *Middle East Journal*, to help research, write, and prepare for conferences or lectures. The internships usually last three to four months and are unpaid except for a small stipend for commuting costs. The positions may be full-time or part-time. All interns may take courses in Arabic, Persian, Hebrew, and Turkish at MEI without charge. College credit sometimes can be arranged upon completion of these courses.

Requirements

Applicants should have an interest in the Middle East and Islam. Some undergraduate work is necessary for the positions.

Application Procedures

Send a cover letter with a resume, a college transcript and a letter of recommendation.

Contact:

> The Middle East Institute
> Kristina Palmer, Internship Coordinator
> 1761 N Street, NW
> Washington, D.C. 20036
> telephone (202)785-1141

MIDDLE EAST NEWS AGENCY

The Middle East News Agency (MENA) is an independent, but government-owned, news organization in Cairo, Egypt. One of its objectives is to focus on news and issues of interest to Egyptians, Africans and Arabs.

MENA offers internships to students interested in journalism. Interns receive practical training and then work for six hours a day as the English deskperson. The internship period is usually four months or less. Interns are paid about $500 per month. Travel expenses, lodging, meals, etc., are the responsibility of the students.

Requirements

Applicants should be recent graduates or college juniors or seniors. Interest in a career as a news agency journalist is important.

Application Procedures

Applications are available from MENA.

Contact:

> Middle East News Agency
> M. Al Biali, Chief of the Board of Consultants
> Hoda Sharawy Street
> Cairo, EGYPT

♻ National Westminster Bancorp Inc.

National Westminster (NatWest) Bancorp accepts summer interns in its offices throughout New Jersey and New York. The highly selective program provides individuals with an in-depth knowledge of a particular area of the bank while allowing them an opportunity to learn about other areas of interest as well.

Each intern is hired for a particular area of the bank, where he or she is assigned a summer project(s). Projects vary, but former interns have learned and utilized financial analysis, LOTUS and other software packages, worked in budgeting, market research and more. Throughout the summer, interns also convene for periodic lectures and seminars covering a variety of commercial banking topics.

Most NatWest summer interns have completed their junior year of college and have a strong interest in learning more about commercial banking. Recruitment begins in the spring, once project needs have been determined.

Requirements

Interns must have some type of living accommodations in the Greater New York area.

Application Procedures

Send a resume and cover letter after mid-April, indicating as specifically as possible the areas of the bank about which you would like to learn more.

Contact:

Manager, College Recruiting
National Westminster Bancorp Inc.
175 Water Street
New York, NY 10038
telephone (212)602-1000

O. S. A. C.

Overseas Schools Assistance Corporation
INTERNATIONAL SCHOOLS INTERNSHIP PROGRAM (ISIP)

The Overseas Schools Assistance Corporation manages the International Schools Internship Program (ISIP) for recent college graduates who want an opportunity to serve as teaching interns in overseas international schools. It is a 10-month internship. Interns gain valuable teaching experience and training by working closely with experienced international educators. They work directly with students in teaching, coaching, tutoring, and supervising extracurricular and other activities.

Interns receive travel costs, a monthly living stipend and health insurance. If they choose, they may earn graduate-school credits toward a master's degree.

Requirements

Candidates need not have majored or minored in education or have teaching experience. Candidates are chosen on the basis of intelligence, the suitability of their personalities for the teaching profession, their level of motivation and interest in teaching overseas, their ability to adjust to living and working overseas, and the specific tutoring, coaching, activities, and academic backgrounds and skills they will bring to the program.

Application Procedures

Write the Overseas Schools Assistance Corporation for an application form.

Contact:

Overseas Schools Assistance Corporation
International Schools Internship Program
445 R West Center Street
P.O. Box 103
West Bridgewater, MA 02379
telephone (508)588-0477

Overseas Development Network

The Overseas Development Network (ODN) is an international, student-based organization committed to educating students and others about global poverty, hunger and injustice. ODN links students with community-based development projects around the world and creates a network of people striving for global grass-roots development. ODN strives to involve students in addressing global problems by providing opportunities for activism and first-hand experience.

ODN's office internship and fellowship programs give individuals an opportunity to learn and actively become involved in global development issues, non-profit management and student organizing. Interns are assigned to a specific project based on the needs of the office as well as the intern's previous experience and skills, aspirations and interests. Examples of projects include development education coordination, international affiliate correspondence, publications research and production, conference organizing, assisting with financial management, membership development and fund raising.

Most internships are unpaid. Work-study funds are available to eligible students. ODN also encourages students of color to apply to the Office Fellowship Program, which offers fellows a monthly stipend. ODN does not provide housing for volunteers.

Requirements

Persons of all ages and backgrounds are urged to apply. Interns should be willing and able to serve as a member of a team, in a cooperative effort to integrate the ideas of all involved. Oral and written communication skills are important and an ability to use Mackintosh computers is very helpful. Most essential is an interest and/or experience in student activism and organizing, and the desire to learn more and educate others about issues related to international solidarity and Third World development.

Application Procedures

There is no deadline for office internship or fellowship applications. People are encouraged to call or write for an application throughout the year.

Contact:

The Overseas Development Network
Volunteer Coordinator
333 Valencia Street, Suite 330
San Francisco, CA 94103
telephone (415) 431-4480

Oxfam America is a non-profit agency that aids in disaster relief and self-help development projects. The organization aids people in Africa, Asia, Latin America and the Caribbean. It also  publishes educational materials on the issues of hunger and development.

Oxfam America uses volunteers in the Boston and San Francisco offices. The volunteers might be involved in clerical support, correspondence, grass-roots organizing or campaign assistance. There also are a small number of work-study placements and individually arranged internships.

Requirements

Volunteers at Oxfam America must live near the Boston or San Francisco offices.

Application Procedures

Send a letter or call to arrange a meeting with the volunteer coordinator.

Contact:

Oxfam America
Wes Callender, Recruitment Coordinator
115 Broadway
Boston, MA 02116
telephone (617)482-1211
fax (617)338-0187

Oxfam America, West Coast Office
513 Valencia Street, #8
San Francisco, CA 94110
telephone (415)863-3981

 Pan American Development Foundation

The Pan American Development Foundation (PADF) is a voluntary organization that strives to promote economic and social development in Latin America and the Caribbean. The organization coordinates programs that provide materials, financial help and technical assistance. Interns are used in the Employment-Generating and Institution-Building Program, the Tools for Training Program and the Health Services Program.

Internships are located in the Washington, D.C., office and may be for a semester or the summer. Interns are expected to work at least 24 hours per week. The positions are not paid. Duties include assisting in project management, preparing reports and performing office duties.

Requirements

Applicants should be undergraduate students or recent college graduates. They should have an interest in Latin America and want to gain experience in development assistance. It is important to have writing or editing experience, computer skills and good communication and interpersonal skills. An ability to speak Spanish or office experience are helpful skills.

Application Procedures

Send a current resume with a cover letter indicating the program for which you would like to work. The PADF sometimes requests personal recommendations or writing samples.

Contact:

Pan American Development Foundation
ATTN: Internship Coordinator, Personnel
1889 F St. NW
Washington D.C. 20006
telephone (202)458-3969
fax (202)458-6316

The Peacemaker Training Institute was organized by the Fellowship of Reconciliation (FOR) to train participants in leadership and international peacemaking skills through academic study, community exposure and service, and hands-on experience. FOR is an activist organization that promotes non-violence. Institute participants are accepted as interns in FOR's national office in Nyack, New York.

Interns work in current FOR program areas, including disarmament, racial and economic justice, youth/campus outreach, local group development, interfaith organization and publications. They help in building action campaigns, raising funds, organization development, media work and publicity, and interacting with international visitors. Interns spend approximately 20 percent of their time participating in seminars and other educational events, 20 percent in local community service and 60 percent in working directly with ongoing FOR programs.

Interns can apply for up to two full semesters of credit toward an undergraduate degree with either Manhattan College or Empire State College. Credit from other institutions may be arranged by the intern. Interns are required to pay room and board expenses, estimated at about $100 per month. This does not include any tuition payments. FOR also can assist in locating part-time employment in the Nyack area.

Requirements

You must be able to make a full-time, nine-month commitment to the program.

Application Procedures

Write for an application form.

Contact:

Peacemaker Training Institute
Fellowship of Reconciliation
Box 271
Nyack, NY 10960
telephone (914)358-4601
fax (914)358-4924

Washington Chapter

THE SOCIETY FOR INTERNATIONAL DEVELOPMENT

The Society for International Development (SID) is a non-political, non-profit, membership organization. There are more than 75 chapters throughout the world. The organization provides programs and publications for those interested in international development to exchange ideas, information and experiences. The Washington, D.C., chapter of SID accepts unpaid interns in full- or part-time positions each semester.

Interns may work on special projects such as the newsletter, coordinating the membership drive, assisting with the annual conference and dinner, or interviewing institutional members. Office duties such as general correspondence, telephone information requests, filing, photocopying and preparing mailings also are part of the internship.

Requirements

Applicants should have a strong interest in international development. Good writing skills, flexibility and a basic knowledge of office procedures also are important.

Application Procedures

Submit an SID intern application to the executive director of the organization.

Contact:

SID - Washington Chapter
Stephen Von Oehsen, Executive Director
1401 New York Avenue, NW
Suite 1100
Washington, D.C. 20005
telephone (202)347-1800

The Summer Institute for Intercultural Communication (SIIC) provides professional training and development to persons who work in multicultural and international environments around the world. The institute conducts several sessions of courses in intercultural topics during the summer. Venues have been at Stanford University and in Oregon. The institute also offers an internship program that lasts about two weeks in July.

The internship program offers an opportunity to explore the discipline of intercultural communication, to assess career directions, and to learn about program design and implementation by working directly with SIIC staff and faculty. Interns work on issues of intercultural education and training, facilitating group process and other concerns. There is strong emphasis on collaborative learning and interns are encouraged to share their experiences. Along with other SIIC participants, all interns attend a section of a workshop titled "Foundations of Intercultural Communication" and a workshop of their choice (the institute offers about 23 workshops). Interns are regular participants in these workshops, in addition to serving as assistants to faculty. In the latter capacity, interns provide logistic support to the workshop and help facilitate communication among participants and staff. Some hosting and services are required, as well.

Interns pay tuition, room and board for the first week of the special internship session, which includes training and participation in the required workshop. Tuition (but not room and board) is waived for the second workshop, in exchange for intern services. Tuition is $600, plus $450 for room and board, totaling $1050. The institute stipulates that being an intern is not a less expensive way to attend a single workshop; rather, it is a chance to get a different and more extensive SIIC experience. Depending on enrollments, interns number from about 10 to about 15.

Requirements

Criteria for selection as an intern are: 1) an intermediate knowledge of the field of intercultural education, training and research; 2) professional experience or graduate student status; 3) commitment to a career in the fields related to intercultural communication; and 4) an enthusiastic willingness to be in a support/service capacity while learning at the institute.

Application Procedures

Resumes and application forms should be submitted by May 15. For an internship application form, contact SIIC for a current brochure. When you receive it, find the SIIC Registration Form in the back of the booklet, check off the box for an internship application, and return the registration form to SIIC.

Contact:

Intercultural Communication Institute
8835 SW Canyon, Suite 238
Portland, OR 97225
telephone (503)297-4622

TRANSAFRICA

TransAfrica is an American lobby for Africa and the Caribbean, with national offices in Washington, D.C., local chapters and 15,000 members across the United States. TransAfrica works to influence the passage of legislation specific to Africa and the Caribbean in the U.S. Congress, as well as general policy attitudes within the U.S. administration and its various agencies. In addition, TransAfrica works to organize and mobilize public opinion around foreign policy issues relating to Africa and the Caribbean. TransAfrica Forum is the educational and research affiliate of TransAfrica. It provides the background research necessary to support the activities of the lobby as well as general education for the public at large on African and Caribbean issues. The Forum publishes a scholarly journal of opinion and occasional in-house research briefs, and hosts an annual conference and periodic seminars.

The purpose of the internship program at TransAfrica and TransAfrica Forum is to provide students with an opportunity to learn, by studying from unique vantage points, the actual formulation and implementation of foreign policy. Interns gain a general hands-on sense of politics in the nation's capital and the process of mobilizing public opinion.

About 11 interns are chosen each semester. All internships are based in Washington, D.C. There are four areas of internship: TransAfrica Lobby; education and research for TransAfrica; development; and administration.

Internships are offered to students from the high-school level through professional school. Students are selected for internships based on their individual interests and backgrounds in conjunction with needs of the organization. Most students arrange to receive academic credit at their educational institutions for the time they spend as an intern. There are no paid internship positions. Students are strongly encouraged to secure adequate financial support and housing for their stay in Washington prior to acceptance of a position.

Requirements

Students interested in TransAfrica internships should be at least college freshmen with a minimum 3.0 overall grade-point average. Students in graduate and/or professional school are encouraged to apply.

Application Procedures

Students interested in obtaining an internship should submit the following materials: a letter of intent that indicates what the student would like to gain from an internship; current resume; brief writing sample (maximum seven pages); and a completed application form. The deadlines for each term are as follows: for fall, August 15; for winter, December 15; for spring, March 15; and for summer, May 30.

Contact:

Administrative Director
TransAfrica
545 Eighth Street, S.E.
Washington, DC 20003
telephone (202)547-2550

US·ASiA

US - ASIA INSTITUTE

The US-Asia Institute was founded in 1979, to promote understanding between the United States and Asia. This non-profit organization engages in research, holds symposiums, coordinates exchanges, and puts out publications focusing on areas that are important to relations between the United States and Asia.

The internship program at the US-Asia Institute has been in existence since 1979. Two to four undergraduate or graduate students are selected each term. Interns work in the Washington, D.C., office. The hours are flexible to suit the students, but most students work 16 to 40 hours per week. Some of the work involved is research, planning conferences or exchanges, attending briefings, tracking legislation, writing, and providing support to the professional staff.

Requirements

Applicants should be undergraduate or graduate students.

Application Procedures

Submit a resume with a written statement (two to three pages) of your goals in serving as an intern and your area of interest in Asia. An additional writing sample may be included, especially something on Asia or US-Asia relations.

Contact:

US-Asia Institute
Mary Sue Bissell, Executive Director
232 East Capital St., NE
Washington, D.C. 20003
telephone (202)544-3181
fax (202)543-1748

The U.S. Chamber of Commerce is the largest federation of business, state and local chambers of commerce, and trade and professional associations in the world. It comprises approximately 180,000 members. In its international programs, the chamber tries to respond to the critical need for global economic and business interdependence for U.S. enterprise. The chamber shapes legislative and regulatory policies at home and abroad that lower barriers and promote open competition. A network of bilateral and multilateral councils around the world complements the chamber's efforts in the United States, and helps produce agreements and shapes trade policies that improve business conditions in other countries.

U.S. Chamber of Commerce Internship Program

The U.S. Chamber of Commerce Internship Program offers a wide variety of internship opportunities on a year-round basis at its Washington headquarters. The program provides opportunities in areas such as production of television and radio shows; researching and writing for a variety of periodicals and special publications associated with international issues and economic policy; legislation and regulations; financial analysis and reporting. Interns working in the international area assist in identification of foreign barriers to U.S. trade and investment; research government policies of debtor developing nations; or research and analyze international trade policy, drafting special reports on trade issues. Internships are unpaid.

Center for International Private Enterprise Latin America Programs Internships

Interns working for the Center for International Private Enterprise Latin American Programs (CIPE) assist in the grant-proposal cycle, which includes analysis of incoming requests for funds and the evaluation of proposed project activities. They also assist in post-funding monitoring and evaluation; drafting of the Latin American sections of quarterly reports; observing and participating in presentations and briefings to representatives of Latin American organizations interested in obtaining CIPE funding; assembling mailings about projects to Latin American groups; and translating documents. Internships are unpaid.

Requirements

You must be a college-level student with good academic standing at an accredited educational institution. All disciplines are eligible for consideration. Interested students should possess good oral and written communication skills and have some working knowledge/familiarity with word processors or PCs.

Those interested in working with CIPE should speak and read Spanish.

Application Procedures

To apply, write to the below address and include a copy of your resume. Specify your area of interest, dates of availability and anticipated date of graduation. In addition, provide your telephone number and the best time to call you during the day. Also include a statement that you understand the internship is without remuneration. Request your career guidance counselor, a faculty member or dean to send a letter of recommendation to the U.S. Chamber of Commerce Intern Coordinator in a separate envelope.

Contact for Both Programs:
Intern Coordinator
Personnel Department
U.S. Chamber of Commerce
1615 H Street, N.W.
Washington, D.C. 20062
telephone (202)463-5732

Visions in Action

Visions in Action is an international non-profit organization founded in 1988 out of the conviction that there is much work to be done in the developing world, work that can be addressed by committed volunteers interested in contributing to social justice and urban development. Visions places interns in Africa to work side-by-side with host-country nationals. The objectives of the organization's Urban Development Internship program are to work towards social and economic justice in the urban areas of the developing world; to raise the consciousness of the public towards global social injustice and the means by which it can be addressed; and to increase public awareness of the culture and contributions of people in the developing nations, by developing educational materials that accurately depict real lives and challenges.

Internships are for one year and are offered in Harare, Zimbabwe; Nairobi, Kenya; Kampala, Uganda; and Johannesburg, South Africa. Interns work for development organizations, health clinics and newspapers as assistant project managers, community development assistants, development journalists, health assistants, low-income housing facilitators, researchers and youth-group coordinators. Ages of interns range from 22 to 50. Participants are from general liberal arts, business, health, technical and scientific fields.

Fees for the internships vary from about $2,000 to $2,900.

Requirements

Some experience relevant to the position is desirable. Positions in broadcast journalism, for instance, are available for those with relevant experience. An ability to learn the local language quickly is desirable.

Application Procedures

You must submit a completed application and two letters of recommendation.

Contact:

Visions in Action
3637 Fulton Street, N.W.
Washington, D.C. 20007
telephone (202)635-7403

THE WASHINGTON OFFICE ON AFRICA

The Washington Office on Africa (WOA) is a church- and trade-union-sponsored, anti-apartheid lobbying and research organization that focuses on South Africa. Founded in 1972, WOA has lobbied on a number of issues, including sanctions, developmental aid and stability of the southern Africa region.

WOA accepts interns in its Washington office on a quarter, semester, summer or year-long basis. Due to staffing constraints, WOA currently focuses on two legislative issues: 1) maintaining sanctions against South Africa, and 2) normalizing relations with the government of Angola. Interns primarily are responsible for tracking legislation related to those issues, working with congressional staff on strategy development, carrying out work related to such strategy, working with WOA's coalition partners in the Southern African Working Group to further the work goals, and maintaining the Africa Hotline, which provides weekly updates about relevant legislation and events in southern Africa. Substantive work pertaining to legislative issues usually involves about two-thirds of an intern's time. About one-third of an intern's time is spent in administrative duties such as photocopying, answering the telephone, delivering messages, taking notes, etc.

Internships are not paid. They are available on a full-time or part-time basis.

Requirements

Interns must be self-starters, motivated and well-organized.

Application Procedures

You must fill out an application form and include an essay.

Contact:

The Washington Office on Africa
110 Maryland Avenue, N.E.
Washington, D.C. 20002
telephone (202)546-7961
fax (205)434-3731

The Washington Office on Latin America (WOLA) is a private, non-profit organization that attempts to influence U.S. foreign policy to advance human rights, democracy and peace in Latin America. The organization is located on Capitol Hill in Washington, D.C., where it holds seminars, sponsors conferences, authors publications, hosts visitors and provides analyses to Congress and the media.

WOLA has unpaid positions for interns interested in Latin America and human rights. Interns are assigned to work with a staff person who monitors a specific country or region. The staff person and the intern set up academic requirements and what is involved in the internship. WOLA has no secretarial support staff, so interns are expected to do some duties such as answer phones, clip newspapers and photocopy. It is preferred that interns work 35 to 40 hours per week, but other hours can be arranged.

Requirements

Applicants should have a knowledge of Latin America and be interested in human rights issues. Good oral and written communication skills are necessary. Spanish is helpful but not required. Applicants also should be able to type or have word processing skills.

Application Procedures

Submit a cover letter, resume, three references and a short writing sample. The letter should state your preference for work on Central or South America and should include a statement that you understand the internship is unpaid. A college transcript may be included, but is not required.

Contact:

Washington Office on Latin America
ATTN: Intern Coordinator
110 Maryland Avenue, N.E.
Washington, D.C. 20002
telephone (202)544-8045
fax (202)546-5288

The Women's International League for Peace and Freedom

The Women's International League for Peace and Freedom is an international organization of grass-roots activists. It has members in 28 countries and in 120 communities in the United States. WILPF women advocate for the equality of all people in a world free of racism and sexism, for an end to all forms of violence and for world disarmament.

WILPF has a year-long internship in Geneva, Switzerland, and New York. It lasts from mid-January to mid-December. January to September is spent in Geneva, where the intern follows human rights activities at the United Nations, contributes ideas, researches information and writes occasional articles. From October to December, the intern monitors the U.N. General Assembly in New York and compiles information.

Travel to Geneva and New York, and housing are provided.

Requirements

Priority is given to women aged 21-35. The candidate must have fluent oral and written English, typing and office skills.

Application Procedures

Send a resume, a 1000-to-1500-word essay explaining your interest in the internship and ideas on how the experience would be used in future work, and two recommendations from non-family members. Applications must reach Geneva by May 15. Applicants are informed by August 15.

Contact:

WILPF Internship Program
Case Postale 28
1121 Geneva 20
Switzerland

 THE WILSON CENTER

The Woodrow Wilson International Center for Scholars was established by Congress as a memorial to the 28th president. Since 1968, there have been more than 1,200 fellows and guest scholars who have used the center to do advanced work in the social sciences and humanities.

The Wilson Center has a 13-week summer internship program. It also offers fall and spring internships for college juniors, seniors and graduate students. The summer program lasts from mid-May until mid-August. Each intern serves as a research assistant for two scholars doing advanced studies. In the summer, interns are required to work 20 hours per week and receive a total stipend of about $520. There are many discussions, seminars and colloquia at the Wilson Center that summer interns are able to attend. The fall internships extend from

September through December, the spring internships from mid-January to mid-May. Interns are required to work between 15 and 20 hours per week. Depending on the number of hours, the stipend is approximately $150 to $200 per month.

Requirements

Applicants may be college juniors, seniors or graduate students.

Application Procedures

Send a detailed resume, two letters of recommendation from faculty members and a transcript. The application deadline is in mid-March for summer interns; August 1 for fall interns; and November 1 for spring interns.

Contact:

The Wilson Center
Zdenek V. David
Smithsonian Institution Building
Washington, D.C. 20560
telephone (202)357-2567

National Capital Service Center
YMCA OF METROPOLITAN WASHINGTON

The YMCA of Metropolitan Washington sponsors an Intern Abroad Program. The program has been in operation since 1982, and places volunteers in YMCAs throughout the world. In 1990, more that 20 YMCAs in Asia, Africa, Europe, the Middle East and Latin America needed volunteers for internships. Many of the assignments are sports-related, but there are some opportunities for teaching (usually English) and community development work. Interns in Australia and New Zealand have helped with sports and camping programs. Zambia has been the site of agricultural projects and refugee programs. In Thailand, the YMCA runs a school where interns teach English. Most assignments are during the summer months, but there are some full-year opportunities. Interns in Australia and New Zealand work only during January and February.

Room and board usually are provided to interns. Costs range from about $500 to $2,500, depending on the country and length of stay. These figures include a $150 program fee, transportation expenses and sometimes food. Some scholarship aid is available for interns from the Washington, D.C., area.

Requirements

Applicants for this program need backgrounds in recreation, sports, agriculture, health, business, English, French or Spanish. Volunteers should be flexible, have a desire to serve others, adapt easily to new environments and have excellent interpersonal skills.

Application Procedures

The YMCA of Metropolitan Washington has updated listings for specific locations, jobs, and length of assignment. Applications and three references are due three months prior to departure.

Contact:

YMCA of Metropolitan Washington
Intern Abroad Program
Holly Dutton, Director
1711 Rhode Island Avenue, NW
Washington D.C. 20036
telephone (202)862-9622

Youth for Understanding (YFU) is an international high-school student-exchange organization headquartered in Washington, D.C. Founded in 1951, YFU is one of the world's largest high-school exchange programs, placing over 3,000 American students with families in 27 countries and bringing approximately 4,000 international students to the United States annually. Sport for Understanding, one of YFU's programs, promotes international understanding through participation in athletics.

Student interns usually work a minimum of 15 hours per week in the Washington headquarters. Interns may arrange to receive credit through their college or university. There are about 13 positions year-round. Some are semester positions, some are summer positions. Interns assist in YFU's various departments in such areas as public affairs, marketing, finance and development.

Work is unpaid, but local transportation costs to and from YFU are reimbursed.

Requirements

Requirements vary according to the internship position. Most positions require good writing and editing skills. Some require computer skills.

Application Procedures

You must obtain and fill out an internship application from YFU.

Contact:

Judy Levy, Coordinator Intern Program
Youth for Understanding
3501 Newark Street, N.W.
Washington, D.C. 20016-3167
telephone (202)966-6808

Section IV

International
Volunteer
Opportunities
With
Private
Organizations

This section lists international volunteer opportunities with non-profit, private organizations. Most positions are unpaid, although some positions and expenses may be paid either partly or wholly by the organization, while some positions entail expenses paid by the volunteer.

Amigos de las Americas

Amigos de las Americas is a non-profit, voluntary organization that sends young public health volunteers to Latin America. The organization was begun in 1965 and has 20 chapters across the United States. Amigos seeks to improve community health in Latin America, improve cross-cultural relations and develop leadership potential in American youth. Latin American countries ask Amigos to develop a summer field program in such areas as animal husbandry, community sanitation, dental hygiene, immunizations, vision health and well digging. Countries planned for future projects include Mexico, the Dominican Republic, Costa Rica, Ecuador, Paraguay and Brazil.

Volunteers are trained to be health workers or receive training for specific projects. At the same time, they are taught Spanish, Latin American history and culture, and cross-cultural communication. Volunteers learn about human relations, management, personal health precautions and safety. Training lasts four to six months and is through the local chapters or by correspondence with the Houston, Texas, office.

The Amigos chapters help to raise money to send volunteers. Volunteers taking the correspondence training receive information on fund raising and are asked to seek donations to pay for their program. The estimated cost of the program is $2,265 to $3,025, depending upon the project site. This fee covers training materials, round-trip air fare from the U.S. departure point to Latin America, field supplies, supervision and some administrative costs. Volunteers are provided with room and board by the host country. Participants are responsible for their transportation to the departure point. Correspondence volunteers must go to Houston, Texas, for a three-day training period before going to Latin America.

Requirements

Participants in the Amigos programs must be 16 years of age or older and have had one year of high-school Spanish. They should want to be involved in improving health conditions in Latin America. Volunteers for this program need to be motivated, independent and self-reliant.

Application Procedures

Send the Amigos application with a $25 application fee. Program sites and dates are finalized in February and the application deadline is March 1.

Contact:

> Amigos de las Americas
> Celdie Sencion, Director of Recruiting
> 5618 Star Lane
> Houston, TX 77057
> telephone (800)231-7796, in TX (800)392-4580
> fax (713)782-9267

Brethren Volunteer Service

The Brethren Volunteer Service (BVS) seeks to promote justice and peace while it serves people in need. The program is sponsored by the Church of the Brethren. Volunteers serve in the United States and in 18 foreign countries in a variety of community service positions. The projects vary widely, but might be in education; health care; prisons; construction; or working with groups like children, the elderly or the homeless. For instance, volunteers in Japan have made visits to victims of the atomic bomb; in Germany they have lived and worked in a community for handicapped adults; and in Nicaragua they have documented Contra atrocities against civilians.

Volunteers for overseas positions must commit to a two-year term of service. Volunteers must attend a three-week orientation prior to their placement overseas. Orientation sessions are held four times a year in various U.S. locations. The cost of transportation to the orientation is the responsibility of the volunteer. The orientation prepares the volunteer to work and live in a different culture as well as to be sensitive to Third World problems. Placement is determined during the orientation. Volunteers make several project choices based upon their skills, interests and location. BVS staff interviews the volunteers and recommends assignments. For some assignments there may be a waiting period before starting, but interim assignments can be made. BVS publishes a booklet that lists current projects and describes duties and requirements.

Room and board are provided, along with round-trip transportation to the project, insurance and a monthly stipend of approximately $35.

Requirements

Overseas assignments require a college degree or its equivalent. Volunteers should be willing to "examine and study (their) Christian faith." Good mental and physical health is a must. The various projects have their own special skill or language requirements.

Application Procedures

An application, medical forms, transcripts, four references, a signed covenant and a recent photo should be received at least six weeks before attending an orientation. The BVS office can supply the necessary forms, as well as give the dates and locations of the orientations.

Contact:

Brethren Volunteer Service
Debra Eisenbise, Recruitment
1451 Dundee Ave.
Elgin, IL 60120
telephone (708)742-5100

The Catholic Medical Mission Board, known as CMMB, was established in New York City in 1928 to support medical missions in developing countries. CMMB places medical professionals in long-term and short-term positions in hospitals and clinics in the Caribbean, Central and South America, Africa, India and Papua New Guinea.

Medical volunteers of all denominations are placed in mission areas, although they must conform to the medical ethics of the mission in which they are placed. CMMB prefers professionals who have completed their medical training and have a minimum of two years of independent experience. General surgeons and general practitioners are most desirable since most mission placements are in primary health care facilities that do not have advanced specialty requirements. CMMB supports surgical specialties in Haiti, where there is an ongoing, five-year program providing health care in one targeted area. Anesthesiologists especially are needed. Nurses and midwives are welcome to apply as are those with educational backgrounds to help train local nurses in state-of-the-art nursing. Some localities do request specialty nurse training, especially with ICE and operating room experience. Dentists are placed in many localities and CMMB supports annual dental visits by teams of dentists and their students in the Dominican Republic.

Only those volunteers who spend at least one year at a mission will receive a minimal stipend with room and board.

Requirements

All applicants should be in good physical condition with the financial resources to provide their own transportation and expenses. Applicants should have an appropriate psychological desire to volunteer for service in an area that often is isolated and extremely undeveloped economically.

Application Procedures

Send a curriculum vitae, including documentation of degrees, medical licensure and registration, and letters of recommendation to CMMB.

Contact:

Catholic Medical Mission Board
10 West 17th Street
New York, NY 10011-5765
telephone (212)242-7757
fax (212)807-9161

Christian Foundation for Children and Aging

The Christian Foundation for Children and the Aging (CFCA) was founded and directed by Catholic lay people to work with poor and abandoned children and aging people through person-to-person assistance programs. The organization has programs in Mexico, Guatemala, Honduras, El Salvador, Nicaragua, Costa Rica, the Dominican Republic, Haiti, St. Kitts-Nevis, Colombia, Venezuela, Peru, Bolivia, Brazil, Chile, the Philippines, India, Kenya, Madagascar and the United States.

CFCA seeks volunteers who are specialists in agriculture, child care, teaching, instructing in health care, nursing, house parenting, social work and nutrition. CFCA volunteers serve as the personal bridge between the children/aging in the overseas country and their sponsors in the United States, Canada, Europe and Australia.

Volunteers receive room and board. Stipends are available in some places. Insurance is provided by the volunteer. Transportation to and from the mission site is provided by the volunteer.

Requirements

Volunteers must have good personal and academic qualifications for the specific professional work to be done. They must be motivated by gospel values to live and work among the poor. Fluency in Spanish is required for placements in Latin America.

Application Procedures

Write for an application.

Contact:

Christian Foundation for Children and Aging
1 Elmwood Avenue
Kansas City, KS 66103-3798

The Citizens Democracy Corps (CDC) collects and disseminates information on U.S. voluntary assistance in Poland, Hungary, Czechoslovakia, Yugoslavia, Bulgaria, Romania and the Commonwealth of Independent States (C.I.S.).

The networking capabilities of CDC's database can be useful to individuals seeking international volunteer positions. CDC's database includes three major information components: information on individual volunteers; information on organizations that currently are involved or want to be involved in voluntary assistance to Eastern Europe; and information on needs or requests for assistance from host-country organizations.

When individual volunteers contact CDC they are sent a four-page questionnaire that covers aspects of academic and occupational backgrounds, linguistic abilities, overseas experience, where the volunteer would like to serve and for how long. When the questionnaire is returned, CDC enters the information into its database. If an organization requests information on potential volunteers for a specific project, CDC can compile a list of appropriate candidates by searching the database.

Although CDC is a networking organization, it is not a placement agency. Its purpose is to function as a clearing house of information concerning voluntary assistance efforts in central Eastern Europe and the Commonwealth of Independent States, and to provide that information to individuals and organizations who request it. CDC neither coordinates volunteer programs nor directly recruits volunteers.

Application Procedures

If you'd like to receive a volunteer questionnaire, or if you or your organization wants to start a volunteer project in Eastern Europe or the C.I.S., write or call CDC.

Contact:

Citizen's Democracy Corps
1815 H Street, NW, Suite 1010
Washington, DC 20006
telephone (202)872-0933, toll-free (800)321-1945.

Community Service Volunteers (CSV) is a national charity in the United Kingdom. Its purpose is to give young people in the United Kingdom the chance to be involved in community action and to help those in need in their own country. The Overseas Volunteers Programme offers the opportunity for volunteers to come to the United Kingdom and serve in various projects.

Volunteers work in hospitals, daycare centers, hostels or even people's homes. The length of service can be from four to 12 months. Summer placements (10-16 weeks) are with the Independent Living Scheme (ILS). Summer volunteers are placed in the homes of people with disabilities, mental handicaps or special care requirements. Duties might involve serving as the "arm and legs" of the person, helping with personal care, cooking or shopping.

The CSV charges a placement fee of about $680 ($235 for the summer program). Volunteers receive housing, food and some pocket money. Housing may be in the person's home or in an apartment nearby. Airfare to London is the responsibility of the volunteer. Volunteers should be prepared to stay on their own in London before they are placed. Volunteers are interviewed and placed when they arrive in London. Placement is usually within two weeks, but in some cases it could take as long as four weeks. Volunteers are responsible for their own room and board during this time (allow about $210-$230 per week).

Requirements

Volunteers should be between 18 and 35 years of age. There are no specific skills needed. Appropriate training and instruction is given each volunteer. You must be willing to accept an assignment anywhere in the United Kingdom. Summer participants may start in June or July and may be required to do some lifting in their assignments. Some projects, especially those working with children, may require the volunteer to furnish a police check.

Application Procedures

Request an application from CSV. There are no application deadlines, but at least two months' notice before your intended starting date is desirable. September and October are the busiest months for placements and there are fewer choices for volunteers at that time of year.

Contact:

Community Service Volunteers
The Overseas Programme
237 Pentonville Road
London N1 9NJ England

CONCERN/America is a non-governmental, international development and refugee aid organization. CONCERN's main objective is to provide training, technical assistance and material support to community-based programs in developing countries and in refugee camps.

Non-salaried CONCERN volunteers serve for at least one year, and are professionals such as medical doctors, nurses, nutritionists, community organizers, public health and sanitation specialists, literacy promoters, etc. In all projects, the focus of the work is on training of local people to carry on the programs, which include providing health care training, developing nutrition or sanitation projects, organizing community development and income-generating projects, conducting literary campaigns, etc. Volunteers currently serve in El Salvador, Honduras, Guatemala, Mexico and Sierra Leone.

Volunteers are provided with room, board, round-trip transportation, health insurance and a small monthly stipend. In addition, a repatriation allowance of $50 per month of service is provided to the volunteer upon completion of contract.

Requirements

Volunteers must be at least 21 years of age and be fluent in Spanish.

Application Procedures

Write CONCERN/America for current volunteer opportunities.

Contact:

CONCERN/America
2024 N. Broadway
P.O. Box 1790
Santa Ana, CA 92702
telephone (714)953-8575
fax (714)953-1242

CSV is a national U.K. charity that places about 2,500 young people in full-time volunteering positions each year, 300 of whom are from overseas.

Applicants can volunteer for up to one year and must have a minimum of four months to offer.

The projects are all across Britain and are wide-ranging, including work with all ages in a wide variety of settings. Some young people arrange with their schools to obtain college credit for their volunteer work.

CSV volunteers do not require a work permit and are supplied with a letter from CSV stating that they are coming to the United Kingdom to be volunteers. This letter is presented upon arrival, when volunteers obtain a visa allowing them to enter the country, subject to the immigration officer's approval.

Volunteers are provided with board, lodging and pocket money. Airfare is not included. A placement fee of about 440 British pounds is required.

Requirements

You must be between the ages of 18 and 35 and be able to offer between four months and one year of your time. You must have an acceptable standard of conversational English. You also must be able to find accommodation and pay to stay in London for three to four weeks before you are placed as a volunteer.

Application Procedures

Send a query letter to CSV.

Contact:

> Overseas Volunteer Administrator
> CSV, 237 Pentonville Road
> London N1 9NJ, England
> telephone 071-278-6601

Education for Democracy
USA

Education for Democracy/U.S.A. (EFD/USA) is a non-profit organization that places volunteer English teachers primarily in Czechoslovakia. Since its inception in 1990, EFD/USA has sent more than 800 American volunteers from all fifty states to Czechoslovakia. In September 1991, it also placed its first volunteers in Latvia and in January 1992 sent its first volunteers to Estonia and Lithuania. EFD/USA has no affiliation with any religious, political or governmental organizations. Its primary source of funding comes from the $50 application fees collected from individual applications. Office space is donated by the University of Alabama in Mobile, though no formal association exits between EFD/USA and the university.

The intent of EFD/USA is to provide primary and supplementary conversational English instruction to people who are interested in learning English or upgrading their existing knowledge and ability, but is in no way intended to supplant any existing language instruction. Generally, students who receive instruction have some foundation in the English language and among them are those students who have reached a reasonable level of proficiency in reading and writing but need practice in verbal communication; however, the levels of language proficiency vary. Instructors teach students and faculty in universities, secondary and primary schools, technical schools, private language schools and a variety of businesses. They must provide their own teaching materials. Effort is made to place instructors in a situation where their educational and professional background can be of assistance; however the emphasis of the program is conversational English instruction. Placements are made according to job availability at the time instructors arrive. Instructors can be placed in a large city or a remote town.

Housing is provided by the employer. This may be in a dormitory, a private home or a small apartment shared with other volunteers. A small monthly stipend equivalent to about $80 is provided by the employer. In Czechoslovakia, medical care is free from the national government. Volunteers also must have their own medical insurance. Instructors must provide their own round-trip transportation to Czechoslovakia. A Mobile, Alabama, travel agency that works with EFD/USA can provide significantly reduced fares.

Requirements

You must be 21 years old and possess a bachelor's degree. You must make at least a four-month commitment, although there is a possibility of extending the commitment beyond the four months up to a year or longer.

The selection process is competitive. Those with experience in teaching English as a second language have priority.

Application Process

You must fill out an application and send a non-refundable $50 processing fee, along with an essay, your resume, two letters of reference and one color photo.

Contact:

Ann Gardner or Ross Phelps
Education for Democracy/U.S.A., Inc.
P.O. Box 40514
Mobile, AL 36649-05145
telephone (205)434-3889
fax (205)434-3731

FOOD FOR THE HUNGRY, Inc.

Food for the Hungry, Inc., seeks volunteers for its Hunger Corps Volunteer Program. The program, which has been described as a "Christian Peace Corps," began in 1979 to address the needs of Southeast Asian refugees at camps in Thailand. Since that time volunteers have worked on projects in 14 countries in Africa, Latin America and

Asia, providing assistance in such areas as agriculture, animal husbandry, primary health care, nutrition, engineering, water resources, physical and occupational therapy, community development and logistics. The following career specialties are sought: water resource engineers, agriculturalists/animal husbandry specialists, nurses/nurse practitioners, nontechnical and administrative personnel, social workers, journalists, English as a Foreign Language instructors, project administrators and computer programmers/trainers.

Those interested in volunteering are invited to Food for the Hungry headquarters in Scottsdale, Arizona, to attend a 10-day orientation covering international development fundamentals, the status of world hunger and strategies for fund raising. Participants then return to their communities to raise money to support their overseas assignments. Once their financial goal is reached, they return to Scottsdale for a month-long training program prior to being sent overseas. Volunteers have the option of choosing which country they will serve in from among those with active Food for the Hungry programs.

Requirements

Volunteers are required to be at least 21 years of age and able to make a three-year commitment. A college degree is required for most positions, although a few opportunities exist for volunteers with equivalent work experience.

Application Particulars

Write Food for the Hungary for more information and application procedures.

Contact:

Food for the Hungry
ATTN: Darla Templeton
7729 East Greenway Road
Scottsdale, AZ 85260
telephone (800)2HUNGER

The Fourth World Movement (FWM) was founded in 1957 by Father Joseph Wresinski after he became chaplain to 252 homeless families living in an emergency housing camp near Paris, France. Determined to end the poverty of these families, Wresinski launched various grass-roots projects with them, and the movement eventually was joined by other friends and volunteers. One of FWM's main missions soon became sending international teams of full-time volunteers abroad to work in partnership with disadvantaged families. The organization now reaches families living in 23 countries on four continents.

Volunteer Program

FWM has more than 300 long-term, full-time volunteers from all over the world. About 20 are from the United States. Every year, from four to 12 new volunteers undertake an in-depth, two-month internship, living and working with full-time volunteers in Washington, D.C., and sometimes in New York City. Those willing to commit to a two-year or longer volunteership then are sent where their skills and interests lie and where FWM most needs them.

Teams of trained, full-time volunteers live within the communities they serve, learning from impoverished families how to work with them to enable them to overcome persistent poverty. The volunteers help run educational and cultural projects and maintain representation at UNICEF and other international organizations, where they serve as witnesses to the courage and endurance of families in poverty. On-site, volunteer teams and disadvantaged families set up programs in ghettos, slums, shantytowns and depressed rural areas. Many of the projects involve education, including preschools, literacy projects, job training and street libraries. FWM also promotes meetings and events that encourage the adults in the families to voice their concerns and to participate in the life of their community. Volunteers write daily about the experiences they witness, recording what the families say. These detailed accounts, which have been collected for over 30 years from many countries, are the basis for evaluating programs, writing documents and representing the persistently poor.

Full-time volunteers are paid minimal stipends.

Requirements

Interns must be 19 years of age or older and have completed high school or have some previous work experience.

Application Procedures

Send a letter of interest. The first step to becoming a volunteer is to participate in a two-month internship. You will live and work with full-time volunteers as you learn about the movement and its approach to persistent poverty. If you then decide on at least a two-year commitment and are accepted, you will continue training and work with a Fourth World team in the United States or abroad. Placement of new volunteers is based on abilities, the needs of the movement and personal preference.

Contact:

Fourth World Movement
7600 Willow Hill Drive
Landover, MD 20785
telephone (301)336-9489

International Work Camps

FWM runs work camps for young people from different countries in Mery su Oise, France. Each work camp lasts for two weeks and three are offered during the summer—one in July, one in August and one in September. The project is constructing FMW's international center. Participants perform various types of manual work, including masonry, painting, electricity, carpentry, secretarial work and cooking. They work seven hours a day. Evenings are dedicated to conversation and reflection on poverty and personal commitment.

Participants must pay all their own expenses.

Requirements

Participants must have medical insurance.

Application Procedures

Write to the FWM office in France for an application.

Contact for Both Programs:

International Movement
ATD Fourth World
107, avenue du General Leclerc
95480 PIERRELAYE - France

Global Volunteers is a non-profit corporation that sponsors short-term volunteer work opportunities in Eastern Europe, Central America, North America, Asia, Africa, the South Pacific and the Caribbean. The work projects are in rural communities and Global Volunteers work on a project or projects where the villagers need assistance. Teams of Global Volunteers have planned and built schools,

built community centers, assisted health care providers, renovated a building for a library, tutored children and identified crop diseases.

The projects are for one, two or three weeks. Volunteers come from all types of backgrounds. Volunteers work alongside villagers and are under the direction of a Global Volunteer team leader and a project manager. Volunteers are sent video tapes and manuals in preparation of their trip. The materials present the culture, history, politics, climate and geography of the host country. Advice such as "do's and don'ts," what to take, and information about health also is presented. The teams meet either at the gateway city or at the point of entry for additional orientation. There may be some language training for teams assigned to villages where little English is spoken.

Trip-related expenses are tax-deductible. A two-week trip to Mexico is about $850, excluding airfare. A trip to Jamaica is about $1,225. The cost for a two-week trip to Guatemala is about $1,300. The three-week trips cost as follows: $1,825 for Poland; $1,150 for Kenya; $1,800 for Tanzania; and $1,775 for Indonesia. These costs include training, visas, ground transportation, hotels, village lodging, food while in the village, project costs and administration fees. Airfare is excluded. Trips are scheduled year-round. Upon returning, volunteers may choose to work with other returned volunteers to provide support to the villages where they lived and worked.

Requirements

Volunteers can be students, professionals, homemakers, farmers, etc. A willingness to make a short-term personal contribution to the development of a rural village is important. All local laws and customs must be honored by volunteers at all times.

Application Procedures

To become a participant, complete an application and a skills inventory check, and sign a waiver of liability.

Contact:

> Global Volunteers
> 375 East Little Canada Road
> Saint Paul, MN 55117
> telephone (612)482-1074 or (800)487-1074
> fax (612)482-0915

ᐟᕦᐠ *Habitat for Humanity International*

Habitat for Humanity is an ecumenical Christian organization that seeks to provide housing in developing countries for those unable to secure adequate shelter on their own.

International Partners

Habitat's International Partners work with future homeowners, or "family partners," in constructing houses. Upon completion of a house, the family for whom it is meant buys it for $1,000-$3,000, with a nonprofit/no-interest mortgage provided by Habitat. The mortgage payments go into a revolving fund that supports the construction of additional houses. Habitat has ongoing projects in Bolivia, Brazil, Burundi, Costa Rica, Dominican Republic, Ghana, Guatemala, Haiti, Honduras, India, Indonesia, Kenya, Malawi, Mexico, Nicaragua, Nigeria, Pakistan, Papua New Guinea, Peru, Philippines, Solomon Islands, South Africa, Tanzania, Uganda, Zaire and Zambia.

International partners serve for a period of three years, including an 11-week training period at Habitat's headquarters in Americus, Georgia. Training topics include construction techniques, intercultural awareness, community organizing and development issues, and project operations. During training the partner and staff determine where the partner will serve, based on the partner's skills, background and current project needs.

Partners receive a monthly stipend, housing and health insurance while in training. Once assigned overseas, they continue to receive these benefits plus coverage of international travel expenses.

Requirements

The only requirements for international partners is that they be at least 21 years of age and have a faith commitment, which need not be Christian. Though not required, Habitat prefers applicants who have knowledge of a foreign language, administration, construction, management or community organizing, and who have experience living or working overseas. A college degree and small-business experience also are desirable. Partners are not involved in pastoral work.

Global Workcamps

Habitat also sponsors one- to three-week intercultural experiences, called Global Workcamps. Groups of volunteers work together to raise funds for a house and travel to the overseas site to construct it.

Requirements

The only requirement is that you be at least 18 years of age.

Application Procedures for Both Programs

To receive more information and application forms for Habitat's international projects, specify the program in which you're interested.

Contact for Both Programs:

Habitat for Humanity International
ATTN: Personnel Department
Habitat and Church Streets
Americus, GA 31709-3498
telephone (912)924-6935

Health Volunteers Overseas (HVO) is a private, non-profit organization committed to improving health care in developing countries through training and education. HVO operates training programs in the Caribbean, Central and South America, Africa and Asia.

HVO seeks medical professionals to volunteer to teach health care

overseas. HVO has volunteer opportunities mainly for physicians, although it occasionally places physical therapists and nurses. Specialists are sought in the areas of anesthesia, dentistry, general surgery, oral and maxillofacial surgery, and orthopedics.

Volunteers are responsible for their own travel expenses and living costs, which usually are minimal. Expenses are tax-deductible.

Requirements

You must be a skilled and experienced health professional from private practice or a university setting.

Application Procedures

You first must join HVO. Annual dues range from $15 to $100, depending on your specialty. Then submit a health volunteers application to HVO.

Contact:

HVO
c/o Washington Station
P.O. Box 65157
Washington, D.C. 2035-5157
telephone (202)296-0928

The Institute of Cultural Affairs

The Institute of Cultural Affairs (ICA) is a private, non-profit, voluntary organization concerned with the human element in world development. Formerly the research division of the Ecumenical Institute, it has been operating as ICA since 1973, designing and applying methods of human development in communities and organizations. Since 1989, national offices of ICA have related through membership in ICA International, Brussels.

ICA Chicago has five volunteer work-study programs: The Space Between, The International Camp for Community Activists, The Village Volunteer Program, Leadership Options, and Residential Urban Internships.

Volunteers must be self-supporting while on assignment as well as cover the costs of their training, orientation, travel, room and board. Depending on the location, volunteers might live in staff housing, training centers or with arranged families. ICA covers expenses of project-related work only.

The Space Between

The Space Between is conducted in conjunction with ICA Peru, ICA Guatemala or ICA Mexico. It offers volunteers a two- to four-week experience in working and interacting with local people while living with village families. It includes field trips for an inside look at the cultural and historical heritage of the chosen country.

The International Camp for Community Activists

The International Camp for Community Activists is a work-study experience conducted in New York, and concluded with a trip to a human-development project in Portugal.

The Village Volunteer Program

The Village Volunteer Program is run through ICA in Brussels. A limited number of volunteers are accepted in national ICAs on the basis of need in each country. They work as part of a team and live under local conditions. National ICAs are looking for people who are mature enough to interact creatively with complex and unpredictable situations. Volunteers undergo training or orientation in the United States (Leadership Options, mentioned below) or Brussels (Village Volunteer Training).

Leadership Options

Leadership Options is a 16-day experience exploring the depressed, underdeveloped community of Uptown, Chicago, where 84 different languages are spoken. Persons considering careers in the voluntary and non-profit sectors can learn first-hand about the challenges faced and methods to meet them. Resources include the urban service agency network as well as the resident ICA staff with their many years of experience in international development and training. Volunteers live in staff housing, training centers or with arranged families, depending on the location. Volunteers must be self-supporting while on assignment as well as cover the costs of their training, orientation, travel, room and board. ICA covers expenses of project-related work only.

Residential Urban Internships

Residential Urban Internships range from three to nine months to fit the needs of the intern, but usually involve voluntary work with ICA or other Chicago agencies while doing special study or research in Chicago, either independently or under the supervision of ICA staff. Participation in Leadership Options or another ICA course is recommended but not required.

Requirements

Two or more years of college are recommended, but graduate students, career-switchers and retirees will find appropriate challenge.

Application Procedures for All Programs

Send a letter of inquiry along with your resume.

Contact for All Programs:

> Institute of Cultural Affairs (ICA)
> 4750 North Sheridan Road
> Chicago, IL 60640
> telephone (312)769-6363

IICD
Institute for International
Cooperation and Development

The Institute for International Cooperation and Development (IICD) is a private, voluntary organization that seeks to help create better world citizens. It sponsors a program called Global Education, which offers volunteer opportunities that allow participants to work and travel overseas.

Volunteers in the program meet people from other countries, talk with them and help them solve their problems. Most of the programs last 12 months, including four months of preparation and language training in Williamstown, Massachusetts; six months of volunteer work overseas; and two months back in the United States, making presentations to interested audiences and producing educational materials. Opportunities also exist for those interested in shorter, summer programs.

IICD offers Solidarity Programs in Angola, Mozambique, Nicaragua and Brazil. Teams of participants work on a community project such as construction or forestation. Involvement in projects also offers opportunities for cultural and educational activities.

In Luanda, Angola, IICD is starting up a school for street children. The program includes documenting the work done and collecting information about Angola and southern Africa. Participants write about, tape and photograph their experiences and the situations they encounter. Three weeks are spent traveling to other parts of Angola.

The IICD program in Nacala, Mozambique, entails working in a forestry project on a plantation. The purpose of the plantation is to produce firewood and wood for construction for local use. The plantation's nursery produces seedlings for the plantation as well as a variety of plants for sale in the community. The project provides jobs for many Mozambicans as well as education and health care specialists. Volunteers document their project as well as the culture, economy and politics they encounter. Some weeks are spent in other parts of Mozambique.

Volunteers in the Nicaragua program live with Nicaraguan families while carrying out a construction project in a rural community. Projects can be construction of a school, a day-care center or a facility for production of building materials for the community. Time is allocated towards traveling and exploring Nicaragua and/or neighboring countries.

The Brazil program lasts only six months, including two months' preparation, three months in Brazil and one month's follow-up back in the United States. In Brazil the group lives in a rural cooperative while working on the construction of an educational facility for cooperative members. The group also has some time to explore the rest of the country.

Academic credit for these programs can be arranged with the participant's school. The fee for the programs is about $4300. Covered expenses include tuition, room, board, traveling expenses, vaccinations and insurance for the period overseas.

Requirements

Applicants should be 18 years of age or older. There are no special skill or educational requirements. Participants should be willing to accept the challenges of being part of a group for nine to 12 months and be willing to open themselves to the cultures around them.

Application Procedures

Send an application form with a $10 processing fee. A personal interview is required to discuss the programs and your needs.

Contact:

Institute for International Cooperation
    and Development
Global Education Program
P.O. Box 103
Williamstown, MA 01267
telephone (413)458-9828

U.S. COMMITTEE
international christian youth exchange

The International Christian Youth Exchange (ICYE) is a non-profit organization that offers international service and cultural-exchange programs to high-school students and young adults. The ICYE seeks to educate young people about global issues and cultural diversity.

Participants are assigned a service project in one of more than 30 countries that participate in the program. Volunteers might work in a day-care center in Norway, be a teacher's aide in Nigeria, or be part of a rural development project in Costa Rica. Almost all of the programs last for a year, starting and ending in July. ICYE also sponsors an International Workcamp Program that lasts from three to six weeks. The program has included ecological projects in Italy and construction projects in Ghana and Kenya.

Living arrangements are made by ICYE in the host country. Volunteers may live with families, at the work site or with others in the exchange program. The fee for the voluntary service program is about $4,750. The fee for work camps ranges from about $2,000 to about $2,700. This includes all international travel, required conferences before and after the program, orientation and insurance coverage while overseas. The host country provides room, board and some spending money. Participants must pay for their own transportation to and from Chicago, passports, visas, etc. ICYE offers scholarships of $250 to participants who find a U.S. family willing to host an exchange. Additional scholarships are available.

Requirements

Volunteers should be 18 to 30 years of age. Knowing the language of the host country is helpful; however, ICYE gives basic language instruction during orientation. Participants should begin language study as soon as they learn their destination. Personal qualities sought by ICYE are adaptability; maturity; concern for world affairs, especially peace and justice issues; a friendly and outgoing personality; and good health. Applicants also should be prepared to study in preparation for their exchange. Applicants are required to have a sponsor. The sponsor can be a local ICYE Committee, parents or guardians, or the actual applicant.

Application Procedures

Send the ICYE application after August 1 for the program starting the following July.

Contact:

International Christian Youth Exchange
Andrea Lee Spencer, Director for Outbound Programs
134 West 26th St.
New York, NY 10001
telephone (212)206-7307
fax (212)463-9824

The International Executive Service Corps (IESC) is a network for volunteers who can provide technical and business management expertise to developing countries and the newly emerging democracies of Eastern Europe and (soon) to the Commonwealth of Independent States. Since its creation in 1964, IESC has completed more than 12,700 advisory projects in 92 countries.

IESC's program in Hungary, for instance, originally focused on the transfer of major government-owned industries to the private sector. This entailed setting up a Budapest Stock Exchange. Future projects in that country likely will be more concerned with the operating and management needs of small businesses. In Poland, IESC has placed U.S. experts to consult on the manufacture of rayon fiber and cellophane and on the production of color television sets.

Volunteers are selected from a "skills bank" and matched with a specific project based on an expressed need of the requesting country. The skills bank contains volunteers for almost every type of business imaginable, from agriculture to retail merchandising, from small firms to large corporations. Most volunteers are retirees who are available for short-term assignments—the average length of an assignment is two months. The average age of an IESC volunteer is 68.

Volunteers receive a per-diem allowance, which allows for comfortable living, but no salary. Round-trip travel for both volunteer and spouse also is provided.

Requirements

You must have experience or training in a business-related field.

Application Procedures

Once your application is on file, you'll be considered for future projects in your professional area. For an application for your name to be placed in IESC's database, send a cover letter and resume to IESC.

Contact:

International Executive Service Corps
ATTN: Recruitment Division
P.O. Box 10005
Stamford, CT 06904-2005
telephone (203)967-6000

the International Eye Foundation

The International Eye Foundation (IEF) was founded in 1961 as the International Eye Bank, a branch of CARE/MEDICO. It was incorporated as the International Eye Foundation in 1969. The organization is dedicated to the promotion of peace through the prevention and cure of blindness worldwide. It plans and implements primary eye care and blindness-prevention programs in less developed countries, with the purpose of encouraging these countries to achieve self-sufficiency in eye health care. It does this by providing training; offering clinical, surgical and preventive services; providing equipment, supplies and medication; and educating the public. Over 60 countries have benefited from IEF programs.

IEF seeks ophthalmologists to volunteer to provide eye care in several developing countries on a short-term basis. There is no stipend, but airfare is provided if the doctor can commit to three weeks or more. Housing and sometimes food and a car are provided.

Requirements

You must be a board-certified ophthalmologist.

Application Procedures

Write or telephone IEF for further information.

Contact:

The International Eye Foundation
ATTN: Ms. Laine Isaacson
7801 Norfolk Avenue
Bethesda, MD 20814
telephone (301)986-1830

 INTERNATIONAL MEDICAL CORPS

The International Medical Corps (IMC) is a private, non-profit organization established in 1984 by U.S. physicians to provide medical assistance and health care training to devastated countries worldwide. Its major goals are to help developing countries become medically self-sufficient. IMC has programs in Afghanistan, Pakistan, Angola and Somalia.

IMC seeks volunteers who are emergency room physicians, family practice physicians, orthopedic doctors, RNs, physicians' assistants and other health workers.

IMC provides housing, a monthly stipend, medical insurance and airfare.

Requirements

You must be a degreed and/or certified health worker.

Application Procedures

Send a query letter and a resume.

Contact:

International Medical Corps
Personnel Recruiting Department
5933 West Century Blvd., Suite 310
Los Angeles, CA 90045
telephone (310)670-0800
fax (310)670-0125

The International Rescue Committee (IRC) is a non-profit, non-sectarian, volunteer agency that provides relief assistance to refugees throughout the world, with health care programs in Thailand, Pakistan, Central America, Malawi and the Sudan. It was founded in 1933 at the request of Albert Einstein, to help anti-Nazis trapped in Hitler's Germany and those escaping to free countries.

Volunteers include doctors, nurses, public health workers, teachers, child care specialists and sanitation engineers. They work in refugee camps, dispensing medical care, teaching preventive medicine, training refugee health workers, drilling wells and promoting self-help programs.

Volunteers receive housing, health insurance and a monthly stipend of $300. Transportation to the work site is not provided. Professional staff members receive transportation and pay of $1,000 per month.

Requirements

Applicants with backgrounds in public health are preferred. For Pakistan, IRC employs professionals with experience in agriculture, construction and administration. All positions require a commitment of at least six months.

Application Procedures

There is no formal application. Just send a copy of your resume with a cover letter informing IRC of dates of availability.

Contact:

Liliana M. Keith
International Rescue Committee
386 Park Avenue South
New York, NY 10016
telephone (212)679-0010

IVS International Voluntary Services, Inc.

International Voluntary Services, Inc. (IVS), was established in 1953 as a private, international development agency. IVS recruits volunteers to serve around the world.

IVS volunteers provide technical assistance to fight against hunger, poverty, and inequality in Asia, Latin America and southern Africa. Volunteers are recruited for two-year postings to work in the areas of agriculture, animal husbandry, community health, nutrition and organizational development.

Volunteers receive a cost-of-living allowance and a stipend.

Requirements

Volunteers must have previous overseas experience and a degree in the discipline in which they will be working.

Application Procedures

Send a letter and a resume indicating your geographical area of interest.

Contact:

International Voluntary Services, Inc.
Recruitment Officer
1424 16th St. NW, Suite 204
Washington, D.C. 20036
telephone (202)387-5533
fax (202)387-4234

For information on IVIS internships, see the section earlier in this book titled "Independent Internships and Traineeships."

Interplast, Inc., was founded in 1965 by Dr. Donald Laub, then Chief of Plastic and Reconstructive Surgery at Stanford University Medical Center. It is an international volunteer medical organization, providing free reconstructive surgery to children and adults in Bangladesh, Bolivia, Chile, Cyprus, Dominican Republic, Ecuador, Honduras, Jamaica, Korea, Lesotho, Mexico, Nepal, Peru, West Samoa, Thailand and Vietnam. In 1991, Interplast sent 26 volunteer  teams (300 medical professionals) abroad to perform 1,600 operations. It also brought 22 patients to the United States for care through its Domestic Program. Interplast has affiliates in Germany, Australia, the Netherlands, United Kingdom, Turkey and Italy.

Program costs vary for volunteers according to medical specialty. Plastic surgeons and anesthesiologists are expected to pay their own airfares and all other expenses. Pediatricians pay on-site expenses. Nurses' expenses are covered by Interplast.

Requirements

The only medical professionals accepted by the program are plastic surgeons, anesthesiologists, pediatricians, operating-room nurses and PACU nurses.

Application Procedures

Plastic surgeons, anesthesiologists and pediatricians should send a current curriculum vitae and cover letter to Interplast. Nurses can request an application from the Interplast office.

Contact:

Professional Services Coordinator
Interplast, Inc.
2458 Embarcadero Way
Palo Alto, CA 94303
telephone (415)424-0123
fax (425)424-8761

✠✠ JESUIT INTERNATIONAL VOLUNTEERS

Jesuit International Volunteers (JIV) is a Christian organization that works for social justice and peace. The organization sends volunteers to live and work in developing nations. Programs have been located in Belize, Central America, Asia, Micronesia and the Western Pacific.

Volunteer assignments are made for two years. Volunteers must live very simply so that they can be more understanding of the needs around them and actually be part of the community where they work. All volunteers are required to assist with fund raising to pay for some of the program costs such as transportation and health care. JIV or the project site take care of all other expenses. Room, board, and a monthly stipend are provided to the volunteer. Attendance at a pre-orientation weekend also is required.

Requirements

You must be 21 years of age or have a college education. You should have transferable skills from a college degree or from work experience. JIV says "Christian motivation" and a desire for a cross-cultural experience are important qualities for volunteers. It also stipulates that a sense of adventure and a sense of humor are necessary.

Application Procedures

Send the pre-application to the JIV office. In November, application packets are mailed to prospective volunteers. Send the application to JIV by March 1. An autobiography, transcript, five recommendations and a personal interview are other application requirements.

Contact:

Jesuit International Volunteers
P.O. Box 25478
Washington D.C. 20007
telephone (202)337-6143

Lalmba is a volunteer relief organization, primarily a medical operation, with clinics in Sudan, Kenya and Eritrea. Lalmba is completely operated by donations, with most of the money going directly to food, medical supplies and equipment. Lalmba runs feeding centers, an orphanage, a medical center, an eye clinic and a prosthetic clinic. It also offers small loans to Africans through a development bank.

Lalmba is dependent on professional volunteers to staff its programs. Its greatest need is for volunteer physicians and registered nurses. Postings are from one to four years and between five to 20 volunteers are sent to East Africa each year.

Lalmba provides round-trip transportation, room and board while in the field, plus life and health insurance.

Requirements

Lalmba does not list any requirements for volunteers.

Application Procedures

Fill out Lalmba's application form. After the application is received, Lalmba usually responds with a telephone call.

Contact:

Lalmba Association
7685 Quartz Street
Golden, CO 80403
telephone (303)420-1810

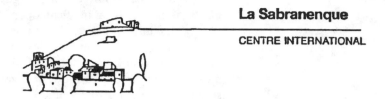

La Sabranenque

CENTRE INTERNATIONAL

La Sabranenque is a non-profit organization that restores abandoned historic sites in France and Italy. It recruits volunteers to work on these sites.

Volunteers work in a multinational team, receiving on-the-job training in traditional building techniques. Work might include stonemasonry, stonecutting, carpentry, floor and roof tiling, path paving or dry stonewalling. The French projects are centered around the village of Saint Victor la Coste, near Avignon. This site dates back to the 11th or 12th century, and La Sabranenque has been working on its restoration since 1969. The program is divided into two-week sessions that start in early June and last through late August. There are also three-week projects, during which participants first spend ten days in Saint Victor la Coste, then go to Italy to work on a restoration site in that country. Italian projects have included restoring monuments, work on a park and farm site, and village revitalization.

Volunteers at the village site in France usually are lodged in the houses restored by La Sabranenque. Meals are eaten family-style. At the Italian sites, living quarters vary from tents to rooms in a local house. At least one day during each session is spent visiting the surrounding region. The cost for a two-week session in France is about $525. The cost for a three-week France/Italy project is from about $920 to about $980. Housing, meals and activities are included in the cost; for the France/Italy projects, the round-trip train transportation from France to the Italian site also is included.

Requirements

No previous experience in restoration work is necessary. Participants should be at least 18 years of age and in good health. Knowledge of some French or Italian is helpful.

Application Procedures

La Sabranenque can provide information on specific projects and dates of the sessions. The application form must be returned with a deposit of $150. This amount can be refunded up to three months prior to the beginning of the session.

Contact:

> La Sabranenque
> c/o Jacqueline C. Simon
> 217 High Park Blvd.
> Buffalo, NY 14226
> La Sabranenque
> rue de la Tour de l'Oume
> 30290 Saint Victor la Coste
> FRANCE

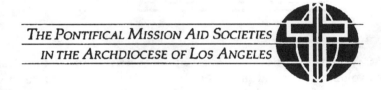

THE PONTIFICAL MISSION AID SOCIETIES
IN THE ARCHDIOCESE OF LOS ANGELES

The Lay Mission-Helpers is a Catholic association of the Archdiocese of Los Angeles. It commissions and trains lay people to serve in missions abroad for a period of three years. It has programs in Kenya, Cameroon, Guam, Thailand, Micronesia and Papua New Guinea. Areas of involvement include education, accounting, medicine, agriculture, skilled trades and secretarial skills.

Volunteers receive room, board, medical insurance, transportation to and from the site, and a small stipend. Prior to departure for their overseas destinations, candidates must participate in an eight-month orientation program in Los Angeles from September to May.

Requirements

You must be a practicing Catholic, a U.S. citizen, have a college degree and/or profession, be willing to make a three-year commitment, and have good mental and physical health.

Application Procedures

Application deadline is September 1.

Contact:

> Lay Mission-Helpers Association
> 1531 West Ninth Street
> Los Angeles, CA 90015-1194
> telephone (213)251-3222

MARYKNOLL LAY MISSIONERS

Maryknoll Lay Missioners is a Catholic service organization that places volunteers around the globe. Lay missioners are involved in a wide variety of works, including pastoral work, health promotion, communications, education, agricultural extension, leadership training and community development. Volunteers serve in Bolivia, Brazil, Chile, Guatemala, Hong Kong, Honduras, Kenya, Korea, Mexico, Nicaragua, Peru, Taiwan, Tanzania, Thailand, Venezuela and the Middle East.

Approximately 40 volunteers are placed per year. They are provided with housing, food, health insurance, transportation, a $150-per-month stipend, a vacation allowance, a $600-per-year retirement pension and a termination allowance of $475 for each year served. A four-month program in language training and orientation is provided. Volunteers must make a commitment for three and a half years, which is renewable. They may request a specific country and most likely will be placed in that country.

Requirements

Volunteers must have experience working with the Catholic Church in the United States. They must have a college degree or a needed skill, followed by one year of work experience. Specialists needed include agriculturalists, journalists, special-education teachers, counselors, lawyers, social workers, economists, pastoral workers, educators and health care professionals.

Application Procedures

Send a letter about yourself: Why do you feel the Lord is calling you to mission overseas with Maryknoll? In what paid or volunteer work have you been involved, both within and outside of the church? What is your educational background? How do you see yourself working in mission? In which areas of the world are you most interested? Include anything else about your background that may be relevant.

Contact:

> Maryknoll Lay Missioners
> Maryknoll, NY 10545
> telephone (914)941-7590

Mennonite Central Committee

The Mennonite Central Committee (MCC) is an international relief and service organization sponsored by the Mennonite and Brethren churches in the United States and Canada. MCC offers several long- and short-term trainee and volunteer programs overseas for young adults.

INTERMENNO Trainee Program

This program places trainees in the Netherlands, Germany, Switzerland and France, for one-year, work-exchange opportunities. Trainees spend the year living and working with European Mennonite families. They work in situations such as households of host families, offices, farms and hospitals or other institutions. Most of the jobs involve manual labor.

Trainees are placed at two different jobs during their stay, each for six months. They have two vacation periods lasting two and a half weeks, and a mid-term conference. A stipend of about $50 per month is provided, along with room, board and some medical insurance. Travel expenses to Europe are paid by the INTERMENNO Trainee Committee of Europe. Participants must pay their own travel expenses to New York City via Akron, Pennsylvania. Trainees depart in August of each year.

Requirements

Applicants should be 19 to 27 years of age and in good mental and physical health. They must be committed to the Christian faith and be willing to be part of the life of the Mennonite church during their stay in Europe. Participants also are asked to study the language of their assigned country during their stay.

SALT International Program

SALT is an acronym for Serving and Learning Together. It is a program that offers work- and cultural-exchange opportunities in Africa, Asia and Latin America. Participants work for a year in farming, business or other industries. Many of the assignments are related to a service program of the MCC. Participants usually work and live with local church members or at a nearby institution. The cost of the program is divided between MCC, the sponsor in the host country, and the participant. SALT participants receive about $47 per month for spending money. The cost for the year abroad is about $2,500. Other expenses are transportation to Akron, Pennsylvania, vacations, a passport, required health examinations and personal items.

Requirements

Applicants should be 18 to 22 years of age and in good health. It is required that all participants be single. A commitment to Christianity is necessary, along with a willingness to be part of the life of the local church and study the language in the assigned country. Participants must be flexible and able to accept the new culture and its social customs. They also should have a recommendation from their home church's leadership.

Canada Summer Service

This voluntary service program assigns young adults to work in resident or day camps, native gardening projects, with the disabled, and on a variety of related projects. MCC publishes an annual list of the summer opportunities available. Previous projects have been in Ontario, British Columbia, New Brunswick, Manitoba and Quebec. Most of the programs run from June through August.

Requirements

Many of the service positions require no special skills. The summer service list published by MCC details any specific requirements.

Application Procedures for All Programs

Application materials are available from the Mennonite Central Committee. Applications for the INTERMENNO Trainee Program and the SALT Program are due by January 15. Applications for Canada Summer Service are due in the spring.

Contact for All Programs:

Mennonite Central Committee
21 South 12th Street
Box 500
Akron, PA 17501-0500
telephone (717)859-1151

Mercy Corps International is a non-profit, Christian, voluntary agency committed to the assistance of the world's poor through emergency relief, self-help development projects and development education. The organization strives to promote self-reliance, productivity and human dignity; seeks to motivate and educate the public about the plight of the poor; and works for peace and justice.

Mercy Corps International regularly recruits agriculturalists and medical personnel, including doctors, nurses, lab technicians, dentists and physician assistants, for its programs in Pakistan/Afghanistan, the Philippines, Sudan and Honduras. The Pakistan/Afghanistan program is a medical-assistance project designed to help three to four million people in 10 provinces in southwest Afghanistan. This project now includes agriculture, irrigation, village reconstruction and survival assistance. The Philippines program includes three major development projects on three islands. In Sudan, the program focuses on food supply and well drilling. In Honduras, the program consists of integrated, community development projects that focus on planting fruit trees, conserving soil and water, and marketing.

Some volunteer positions are unpaid. Medical personnel in Pakistan receive a $575-per-month stipend, round-trip transportation, room and board, medical insurance and "R&R."

Requirements

Medical volunteers should have medical education/certification and a minimum of three years' work experience in the medical field. Agriculturalists must have a B.S. in agroforestry or agriculture.

Application Procedures

Send a query letter and resume.

Contact:

Mercy Corps International
3030 S.W. First Avenue
Portland, Oregon 97201-4796
telephone (503)242-1032
fax (503)223-0501

Mobility International USA (MIUSA) is a non-profit organization whose purpose is to promote and facilitate opportunities for people with disabilities to travel and participate in international exchange programs. MIUSA is the U.S. office of Mobility International, which is headquartered in London. The organization coordinates international educational programs, publishes books and a newsletter, produces videos, provides travel information and referral service to its members, and helps individuals apply to international work camps and international educational exchange programs. It also offers student internships.

MIUSA sells a resource book, *A World of Options for the 90s: A Guide to International Exchange, Community Service and Travel for Persons with Disabilities,* which outlines international opportunities for the disabled. The book is available for $14 to members of MIUSA, or $16 to non-members. As well as helping members apply to work camps overseas, MIUSA hosts its own work camp in Eugene, Oregon, which brings together disabled and non-disabled persons from around the globe to work on a community service project for two to four weeks.

Requirements

MIUSA serves all disabled people, but you need not be disabled to join. Membership in the organization, which entitles you to its referral service, is $20 per year.

Application Procedures

Write to the organization, specifying what kind of a program you are interested in.

Contact:

Mobility International, USA
P.O. Box 3551
Eugene, OR 97403
telephone (503)343-1284 (Voice and TDD)

The National Central America Health Rights Network (NCAHRN) is an organization of health care workers and others concerned with health and human rights in Central America. Its projects and activities include the publication of a newsletter and a quarterly journal on health in Central America and throughout the world; sponsoring regular investigative delegations to El Salvador, Guatemala and Nicaragua;  sponsoring groups to help build and staff health clinics, hospitals, clean water and· nutrition projects, and to train health professionals and community health promoters in Central America; sponsoring symposia and speaking tours for mental-health professionals; and providing material aid to Central America in the form of medical equipment and supplies.

The Training Exchange/NICARAGUA

In its Training Exchange/NICARAGUA program, NCAHRN sends 10 to 20 physicians and nurses each year to medical schools in Leon and Managua, Nicaragua. These doctors and nurses spend two to 12 months working with faculty to develop effective curricula in areas related to primary care.

Requirements

Applicants must be qualified physicians or nurses.

Application Procedures

Write directly to the Training Exchange for application materials.

Contact:

The Training Exchange
c/o David Egilman, MD, MPH
90 West Street
Foxboro, MA 02035
telephone (508)543-3848

The El Salvador Health Training Project

The El Salvador Health Training Project places 10 to 12 medical volunteers per year at the University of El Salvador (UES) School of Medicine, to work with faculty and train the trainers of health promoters in community health projects. They are required to send monthly reports of their work for review by the NCAHRN advisory committee and to participate in fund raising for the program, by writing letters about their work that can be used as fund appeals. The length of placement ranges from six months to two years.

Volunteers receive airfare, room and board, a modest stipend and health insurance.

Requirements

Volunteers must have completed their medical training and be licensed fully in their area of specialty. They also should be fluent in Spanish or plan on achieving fluency by the time of placement.

Application Procedures for Both Programs

Write directly to the network, requesting application materials.

Contact for Both Programs:
Louise Cohen
National Central American Health Rights Network
11 Maiden Lane, Suite 10D
New York, NY 10038
telephone (212)732-4790

OPERATION CROSSROADS AFRICA, INC.

Operation Crossroads Africa, Inc., was founded in 1957, by the Reverend James H. Robinson. The major goal of this non-profit organization is to improve relations between North Americans and the peoples of Africa and the Caribbean. Crossroads offers a variety of oportunities to assist in the development of Africa and the Caribbean as well as to foster international understanding.

The Africa Program

The Africa Program consists of community work-camp projects that usually involve physical labor for several hours each day. Typically, eight Americans and a leader live and work with community members. Living is simple, with basic amenities, and responsibilities for daily maintenance activities are shared by all. The program lasts for seven weeks, including three days of orientation in New York City. About five weeks are spent at the work site, and the remaining time is allotted for group travel, which may be within the assigned country or to nearby countries. Projects are conducted in east, west, south and central Africa. The four major types of projects are community development, agriculture/farming, archaeology/anthropology and medical projects.

A typical community development project might be helping to build a health center or shelters for the disabled, or a village school. The agriculture projects involve clearing land, planting or harvesting. For archaeology and anthropology projects, teams are made up of professionals from the host country and the United States—volunteers help to photograph or survey sites, map areas and collect oral histories. Medical project teams are made up of students and professionals. They provide basic health care and health education projects.

Some opportunities exist for college students in pre-med, public health or counseling to work with African health professionals in community health programs. Students receive an orientation upon arriving in Africa. About four weeks are spent on projects in these general areas: community health; diagnosis and treatment of tropical disease; prevention of tropical disease; and observation of traditional health care. The remaining time is spent in writing reports and on oral presentations.

The fee for the Africa Program is $3,500. Many participants find financial assistance through colleges, churches and other organizations. Crossroads offers assistance in fund raising and is able to offer small grants.

Most participants earn college credit for their work.

Requirements

Applicants must be at least 18 years of age and should have an interest in learning about another culture. Qualities that are important include flexibility, patience and a willingness to contribute to the communal life of the group.

Application Procedures

An application may be obtained from colleges or the Crossroads office. Applications are due by February 15, but early application is encouraged.

The Caribbean Program

The Caribbean Program provides experiences for American high-school students in the Caribbean. The students, under the supervision of an experienced leader, work on a project with teenagers from the host country. The program seeks to enrich the students culturally by giving them an in-depth experience.

Program participants live together in a group situation, or with local families. Accommodations and food are typical of that of the host community. Responsibilities for household chores are shared by the group.

Volunteers are given an intensive, two-day orientation program in New York, just prior to departure. Projects last for six weeks and usually run from late June until mid-August. The cost of the program is $2,500.

Requirements

This program is designed for high-school students who wish to live in and learn about a different culture. They also should be interested in community service and have a willingness to share and the ability to accept new ideas and customs.

Application Procedures

To receive information or applications on programs offered by Crossroads Africa, write the organization, specifying the program in which you are interested.

Contact for Both Programs:

Operation Crossroads Africa, Inc.
475 Riverside Drive, Suite 242
New York, NY 10015
Telephone (212)870-2106

Our Little Brothers and Sisters was founded by Father William B. Wasson in 1954. It runs homes for orphaned and abandoned children in Mexico, Honduras and Haiti. It also provides educational opportunities for these children in Miacatlan, Mexico; Cuernavaca, Mexico; Monterrey, Mexico; Honduras; Haiti; and at an English Language Center in Yarnell, Arizona. The organization considers itself to be a family, thus none of the children involved are eligible for adoption.

Our Little Brothers and Sisters accepts volunteers to work in many different capacities, such as caring for small children or working in offices.

Requirements

There are no basic requirements.

Application Procedures

Send a letter of inquiry to the organization.

Contact:

Nuestros Pequeños Hermanos
Attention: Volunteer Coordinator
Apartado Postal 30-500
06740 Mexico 4, D.F.
Mexico
telephone (602)427-3339 (in Yarnell, Arizona)
fax (602)427-6516

SCI SERVICE CIVIL INTERNATIONAL

Service Civil International (SCI) is an international organization that promotes peace and international understanding by sponsoring work camps. It was begun in Europe in 1920, and today exchanges volunteers in more than 30 countries. SCI-USA provides many opportunities for volunteers to meet and work with other volunteers from all over the world. Programs are available in Europe, North America, Asia and Africa.

Volunteers live and work together and share housekeeping chores. Projects involve manual labor under the direction of a community sponsor. Work camps in Europe and North America last from two to four weeks. In Africa and Asia, some three-month assignments are available. Longer assignments (up to two years) occasionally are available in Europe and the United States. Most of the work camps take place from July to September, but a few take place during June, October and the winter months.

Volunteers must pay all their own transportation and personal expenses. SCI provides room, board and insurance for the duration of the work camp. An application fee of $35 covers placement in a U.S. work camp; $75 is required for longer terms or abroad; and $100 is required for placement in Africa or Asia. These fees include membership in SCI-USA.

Requirements

Applicants for U.S. work camps must be 16 years of age or older. Those wanting to go abroad for a short-term camp must be at least 18 years of age. Volunteers for projects in Africa and Asia must be at least 20 years of age and have had previous work-camp experience.

Application Procedures

SCI-USA publishes a list of international work camps, which costs $3.00. This list is available in April, but you can pay ahead to reserve a copy. To receive information on work camps in the United States, send a self-addressed, stamped envelope.

An application is included with each of the above lists. Send the application with the application fee as soon as possible, since summer placements begin in early May. Volunteers for summer Africa and Asia projects must apply before February, and for winter projects before August.

Contact:

Service Civil International
c/o Innisfree Village
Rt. 2, Box 506
Crozet, VA 22932
telephone (804)823-1826

SHERKIN ISLAND MARINE STATION

Sherkin Island Marine Station is a privately-run, research operation located in Cork County, Ireland. Its main research projects are seashore monitoring and plankton research. Other projects involve seals, birds, insects, butterflies and moths.

The station recruits volunteers to assist in its projects and to help with the general operation of the station. Part of the duties include guiding school children and other visitors to the island. Everyone is expected to help in the garden and with housekeeping chores. Volunteers stay in a bunkhouse with sleeping bags. There is running water, electricity and showers. The station asks that volunteers come on a trial basis for one month due to the roughness and closeness of the living conditions. Volunteers work from March until November of each year.

Volunteers receive room, board and a stipend of about $17.50 per week.

Requirements

Applicants should have an undergraduate degree. Accuracy in keeping records and specimens is essential. Volunteers may be away from the station only for one week during their stay.

Application Procedures

Send a letter of inquiry, with dates of availability, and a resume.

Contact:

> Sherkin Island Marine Station
> Sherkin Island
> County Cork, Ireland
> telephone 353-28-20187

Volunteers For Peace, INC.

"INTERNATIONAL WORKCAMPS"

Volunteers for Peace (VFP) is a non-profit corporation established in 1981 to help promote international cooperation through voluntary participation in work camps in the United States and abroad. Each year VFP coordinates over 800 international work camps in more than 30 countries.

The work camps last from two to three weeks and involve 10 to 20 volunteers from at least five countries. The projects are determined by United Nations-sanctioned organizations and involve construction, restoration or maintenance for a social, environmental or agricultural improvement. For instance, many work camps in Europe involve the restoration of historic buildings such as churches, museums or castles.

Volunteers live together, sharing responsibilities for cooking and scheduling of evening activities.

The cost to participate in a work camp is $125 for all countries except those in the Commonwealth of Independent States, which cost $400 to $700. Volunteers may register for multiple work camps in the same or different countries, but must arrange for their own transportation from the United States and between work camps. Room and board are provided.

Requirements

There is no age limit, but volunteers must be at least 18 years of age for most work camps. Limited opportunities exist for 16- to 18-year-olds in France, Germany and Spain. Proficiency in a foreign language is not required.

Application Procedures

Each April VFP publishes an international work camp directory, titled *The International Workcamper*. The directory lists the current year's camps, including such information as work site, project goal, number of participants, time of year and duration of the work camp. The cost of the directory is $10. After the directory comes out, volunteers register for the work camps of their choice on a first-come, first-served basis. While work camps are held year-round, 90 percent are scheduled from July through September.

Contact:

Volunteers for Peace
43 Tiffany Road
Belmont, VT 05730
telephone (802)259-2759

Volunteers for Tau is a program sponsored by the School Sisters of St. Francis. The School Sisters of St. Francis is a U.S.-based, international community of 2,000 women serving in the United States, Central and South America, Europe and India.

These volunteers serve in education, health care, pastoral ministry, social service and other professions touching human needs. They may work in a hospitality house, a senior citizens' residence, a rural parish, a school for exceptional children, a nursing home, a correctional center, a rural health clinic or a children's crisis center. The length of a volunteership may be from one to six weeks, a month, several months or a full year.

Room, board and travel costs at a work site are provided by the work site or by Volunteers for Tau. Volunteers are responsible for personal and recreational costs; health, accident and car insurance; medical, dental and optical bills; and transportation to and from the site. There is a registration fee of $10.

Requirements

Applicants must be 18 years of age or older, female and single. They must be willing to participate in an alternate lifestyle and shared prayer, be assertive and possess leadership qualities.

Application Procedures

Applicants must complete and return to the volunteer coordinator an application form indicating area of interest and letters of recommendation from their employer, teacher and priest. Those accepted choose a site from a list of options, then complete, sign and return the contract with the $10 registration fee.

Contact:

Coordinator of Volunteers for Tau Program
900 North Street
Omaha, NE 68114
telephone (402)391-4300

Volunteers in Asia (VIA) was started by a group of Stanford University undergraduates in 1963. The goal was to start a program to give first-hand experience in Asia. Today volunteers serve in Indonesia, Japan, Taiwan, Vietnam and the People's Republic of China, teaching English as a second language.

Volunteers In Asia

In Indonesia, undergraduates may teach for a summer or one year. Assignments are in institutions that need English instruction for their staffs. Graduate posts, which require a two-year assignment, usually are for teaching at an Indonesian university. Some graduate students are used as English resource persons for community development organizations. Volunteers in Taiwan teach at YMCA community centers and stay with Taiwanese families. Undergraduates go for six months or one year, while graduate students work for one year. In Japan, there are opportunities to teach English in medical schools or in rural high schools. The assignments in the People's Republic of China are at technical institutes. The Japan and China programs can be for six months or one year. Volunteers go to Vietnam for two years.

Volunteers begin preparation in the winter before their assignment. VIA offers cross-cultural training, teacher training, language study, etc. The host institution provides room, board and a stipend. The fee for the six-month and one-year programs is approximately $990. This includes transportation, training and a week-long program in Japan. The two-year program in Indonesia costs about $305. For these volunteers, VIA pays round-trip transportation and provides medical insurance. Basic costs in the field also are covered. Academic credit can be arranged for the teaching assignment.

Requirements

Applicants must attend a personal interview at Stanford or UC Santa Cruz in January. They must live in the San Francisco or Santa Cruz area during the training period from February to June. They must be undergraduate or graduate students.

Application Procedures
VIA holds recruitment meetings in the San Francisco and Santa Cruz areas. Applications are due in early January.

Contact:

Volunteers in Asia
P.O. Box 4543
Stanford, CA 94309
telephone (415)725-1804

Volunteers in Overseas Cooperative Assistance (VOCA) is a private, non-profit organization assisting cooperatives and agriculturalists abroad. During its 21-year existence, 600 VOCA volunteers have provided assistance in 85 countries on about 1,100 projects and to almost as many organizations.

VOCA enlists senior-level experts from the U.S. cooperative and credit-union fields for short periods of usually 30 to 90 days to help carry out its projects. These experts include specialists in all aspects of agribusiness—farmers, dairymen, extension agents, plant physiologists and veterinarians. They also include specialists such as lawyers, accountants, bankers, CEOs and senior managers. Volunteers work in developing countries (in Africa, Asia and the Near East, Latin America and the Caribbean), in the emerging democracies of Central and Eastern Europe (such as Albania, Bulgaria, the Czech and Slovak Federal Republic, Hungary and Poland), the Baltics (Estonia, Latvia and Lithuania) and the Commonwealth of Independent States.

VOCA activities are in three major areas: cooperative assistance, a farmer-to-farmer assistance program, and assistance to emerging democracies. In the cooperative assistance program, VOCA interns help in the organizational development and improvement of member services for all types of cooperatives. Projects have included conducting a feasibility study to establish a cooperative bank in Zimbabwe; conducting agribusiness seminars in Hungary; training workers in computer operation and application in Bolivia. In the farmer-to-farmer program, volunteers provide technical assistance to small- and medium-sized agricultural enterprises in production, post-harvest handling, processing, marketing, and extension and institutional development. Projects in this program have included advising a beekeepers cooperative on honey production and management in Indonesia; training farmers in identifying and treating diseases common to greenhouse plants in Egypt; and exploring appropriate ways to adapt machinery to harvest the vernonia bean in Cost Rica. Assistance to emerging democracies includes help in developing private agribusinesses and support to private farming. Examples of projects include advising on privatization plans for enterprises in the Czech and Slovak Federal Republic; advising on draft language for Bulgaria's new cooperative law; and conducting marketing seminars in Poland.

VOCA and the requesting organization in the foreign country cover all volunteer costs, including travel, lodging, meals and work-related expenses. Volunteers incur no costs in connection with their assignment. For assignments of more than one month, VOCA arranges for spouses to accompany volunteers. Spouses also may accompany volunteers on shorter assignments, but in that case, the volunteer must pay all of the spouse's travel and other expenses.

Requirements

In general, VOCA volunteers must have expertise related to either cooperative development or agriculture, extensive professional experience in their area of expertise, and the ability to work with people from different cultures and at different stages of professional development. Overseas experience and foreign language ability are not required. Some of the skill areas in which VOCA commonly seeks volunteers include cooperative agribusiness development/management, livestock management, farm management, plant production and protection, food processing, agricultural extension, agricultural marketing, and agricultural credit and finance.

Application Procedures

For more information about volunteering, contact VOCA Program Coordinator Rich Boni or Program Recruiters Carl Hammerdorfer, Jenny Hughel, Cristine Nardi or Tim White at the address below.

Contact:

VOCA
50 F Street, N.W., Suite 1075
Washington, D.C. 20001
telephone (202)383-4961
fax (202)783-7204

Winant-Clayton Volunteers, Inc.

The Winant-Clayton Volunteers, Inc., has sent American volunteers to Britain every summer since 1948. Its original purpose was to help rebuild bombed-out buildings in London. Today volunteers might serve in shelters for the homeless, work with teenagers, help run day camps, or work in a hospital for the handicapped. Many placements are in London, but some volunteers have worked in Liverpool and Scotland.

Volunteers meet in New York City for an orientation program led by a former volunteer. The group then travels together to Great Britain. The group departs in mid-June and returns in late-August. The work lasts six to seven weeks and two to three weeks are reserved for independent travel. All volunteers are required to travel back to the United States with the Winant group. Room and board are provided for the work portion of the program, but volunteers must pay their own expenses for the travel time. All transportation costs are the responsibility of the volunteer. Estimated costs, including airfare, are about $1,500. The Winant Program offers some financial aid for transportation expenses.

Requirements

Applicants must be at least 18 years of age. They must be energetic, enthusiastic, motivated and very flexible.

Application Procedures

Send two application forms (an original and a copy) with a $15 application fee by January 31. Two references also are required. Students should have one reference from a teacher or adviser and one from someone for whom they've worked (salaried or volunteer). Others should submit one reference from their employer and another from a clergyman, teacher, etc. A personal interview with all applicants is required. Notification is made in mid-March, and successful applicants then must pay a $100 non-refundable deposit.

Contact:

Winant-Clayton Volunteers, Inc.
Virginia Peters, Coordinator
109 East 50th Street
New York, NY 10022
telephone (212)751-1616, ext. 271

WorldTeach is a program of Harvard University's social service organization, the Phillips Brooks House Association. It was founded in 1986 with the goal of contributing to education overseas and creating opportunities for North Americans to gain experience in international development. The administration of the program is financed mainly by participants' fees, with additional contributions from the Harvard Institute for International Development, the Phillips Brooks House Association, Harvard University, foundations and individual donors.

Since 1986, WorldTeach has placed over 400 volunteers as teachers in Africa, Latin America, Central Europe and Asia. Most volunteers teach English as a second language, but science and math teachers are greatly needed in Namibia.

In addition to year-long programs, undergraduate and graduate students can participate in a summer program in China, the Shanghai Summer Teaching Program. In this program volunteers spend seven to eight weeks teaching Chinese high-school students in an intensive summer language camp. Volunteers spend each day teaching, participating in cultural activities and learning the Chinese language.

Volunteers pay a program fee of about $3,000, which covers the cost of airfare, health insurance, orientation and training before service, and support during the year. The school provides housing and a small monthly stipend, usually equal to the pay that a local teacher with similar qualifications receives. Student loans can be deferred while volunteers teach, and limited, need-based financial aid is available.

Requirements

No special language skills or teaching experience are required. Applicants are accepted from all majors, but must have a bachelor's degree from an accredited college or university by their date of departure for the one-year programs. Applicants are accepted from all ages and nationalities.

Application Procedures

Most country programs have several departures a year. Application deadlines generally are four months before the date of departure, but admissions are conducted on a rolling basis and applications are accepted at any time. Applications for the summer program usually are due by March 1.

Contact:

WorldTeach
Harvard Institute for International Development
One Eliot Street
Cambridge, MA 02138
telephone (617) 495-5527

Section V

Miscellaneous Work Opportunities

This section lists miscellaneous work opportunities that are not strictly internships or volunteer positions, but that also are of interest.

The Atlantis-Norwegian Foundation for Youth Exchange sponsors a "Working Guest" program. The program is a cultural exchange that places young adults with Norwegian families for one to three months. Participants work for the host family for no more than 35 hours per week and receive room, board and spending money in return. Many of the opportunities are on farms, doing work such as feeding livestock, making hay, or picking fruits and vegetables. In some families, the working guest does housework or has child-care duties.

Atlantis charges a registration fee. Working guests are covered by the Norwegian national health service, but participants should provide their own travel insurance. All transportation expenses are paid by the participants.

Requirements

Applicants must be 18 to 30 years of age and should be ready to work hard. It is desirable but not necessary to have farming experience. Working guests are required to obtain a work permit and a tuberculosis test when they arrive in Norway. Agricultural workers and their luggage must go through a disinfection upon arriving.

Application Procedures

Write to Atlantis to receive an application form. Return the completed application with a medical certificate, a personal reference, a photo and the registration fee.

Atlantis contacts participants about four to six weeks before arrival. A contract confirms the placement with a host family. All other necessary travel plans and dates are worked out by the participants and the host family.

Contact:

Atlantis-Norwegian Foundation for Youth Exchange
"Working Guest" Program
Rolf Hofmosgate 18
N-0655 Oslo 6, Norway

AuPair/Homestay USA/-Abroad is a program of the Experiment in International Living. The program places young Americans in homes in Austria, France, Greece, Italy, Germany, Norway, Spain and Great Britain, to provide 30 to 35 hours of child care per week. Duties include baby-sitting, playing with the children, helping the children with their homework, speaking English with the children, ironing and doing light housekeeping.

Proficiency in the local language is required in France, Germany and Spain, but in general there is no language requirement for other countries. Au pairs stay for at least three months, although host families usually prefer that they stay for 10 to 12 months. Flexible lengths of stay can be arranged and each au pair has the option to extend the stay once placed.

Each host family is required to provide full room and board to the au pair, as well as to pay a stipend in the local currency equal to $200 to $300 per month. They must allot the au pair up to six hours per week to attend classes, and share their culture and language with the au pair.

There is a non-refundable application fee of $75 and a program fee of $1,000. Insurance costs $28 per month. The program fee does not include the cost of transportation, tuition or a visa/work permit.

Requirements

Applicants must be between 18 and 26 years of age, high-school graduates, and experienced in baby-sitting or other child care. They must be flexible and have a good sense of humor, be committed to cross-cultural learning, love children and have a spirit for adventure.

Application Procedures

Send a query letter to the organization, requesting an application form.

Contact:

> AuPair/Homestay Abroad
> 1015 15th Street, N.W.
> Suite 750
> Washington, D.C. 20005
> telephone (202)408-5380

The Council on International Educational Exchange (CIEE) is a non-profit, student-exchange organization. It offers a Work Abroad Program that allows students to work temporarily in other countries without the hassle of the governmental red tape usually involved in acquiring a work visa. The countries that have agreements with CIEE are Britain, Ireland, France, Germany, New Zealand, Costa Rica, Canada and Jamaica. Most of these countries have high unemployment and normally do not award work visas to unskilled foreigners.

For example, in Britain, CIEE works with the British Universities North American Club (BUNAC), offering a program that arranges temporary work opportunities for American students in Britain, and for British students in the United States. This program is called the Student Exchange Employment Program (SEEP). American participants in SEEP receive a special blue card, or work permit, that enables them to seek employment anywhere in England, Scotland, Wales or Northern Ireland for six months maximum, at any time of year, in any type of job. Employment may be found through BUNAC's listings or personal contacts. In 1990, 4,600 students found jobs in Britain as diverse as pub worker, BBC production assistant, banker and busboy. Most students work in secretarial or service jobs, but anything is possible. Wages are the same as for British workers, so students should be able to cover day-to-day living expenses.

SEEP participants receive a program handbook that advises on finding jobs and provides contacts. Twenty-four percent of the 4,600 participants in the 1990 SEEP program pre-arranged jobs before arrival in Britain. Some found jobs through the BUNAC handbook, others through personal research or contacts. Most arrived in Britain with no job set up. On average it takes only three days to secure a job if you are flexible and prepared to accept menial work. Employers are listed with BUNAC at their own request.

BUNAC also has extensive accommodation listings. Almost all BUNAC students live in house-shares or flat-shares found after arrival in Britain. Guaranteed discount accommodation is available for the first few nights in London. The program fee is $96. Participants must provide their own transportation and miscellaneous expenses. Wages should cover living expenses, although it is recommended that participants take at least $500 to cover initial expenses.

Requirements

Participants in all country programs must be college or university students.

Application Procedures

Applicants for all country programs must submit a completed and signed application form; proof of student status; two passport-size photos signed on the back; a completed reference form or a letter of recommendation from a college instructor or recent employer or a written offer of a job from a foreign employer; and the $96 administrative fee.

Contact:

CIEE (Work Abroad Program)
205 East 42nd Street
New York NY 10017

EARTHWATCH

Earthwatch is a membership organization that organizes international expeditions and events for its members. Members serve as volunteers on a project, usually having to do with archaeology or the environment, and pay all their own expenses. For example, an Argentine archaeologist may need volunteers to help locate the settlement upon which Buenos Aires grew. Or a Wyoming mammalogist may need help to undertake a bighorn census in the Rocky Mountains.

Expeditions may last a week, a month, or as much time as you have. Expedition costs are kept low by sharing with other team members and are 100 percent tax-deductible. Expeditioners stay in inexpensive hostels, dorms, private homes or campgrounds, and eat local food. Costs vary with the expedition and length of stay. The annual $25 membership fee, which qualifies you for any and all expeditions, also entitles you to receive *Earthwatch Magazine* and attend invitational events in your local area.

Requirements

All that is required is a $25 membership fee.

Application Procedures

Simply send the $25 application fee to Earthwatch.

Contact:

Earthwatch
Membership Services
P.O. Box 8037
Syracuse, NY 13217

InterExchange is a private, non-profit organization that has been involved with international educational exchange for over 20 years. Its goals are to promote international understanding through intercultural, educational and work/training opportunities. Over the years, through cooperation with many foreign non-profit organizations and government agencies, InterExchange has placed thousands of students both in the United States and abroad.

Following are the overseas work/training programs offered.

France: Grape Picking

Students may sign on for grape-picking jobs that last eight to 10 days, from the end of September into October. These jobs can be hard work physically, but are not difficult to learn. A typical work day (rain or shine) involves picking for four hours in the morning, breaking for lunch, and then picking for four hours in the afternoon. In some cases, students may be able to participate in harvesting at more than one vineyard.

Room and board are provided in addition to a daily salary. There is a program fee of $50, plus additional placement fees to be paid upon arrival in Paris.

Requirements

Applicants must be full-time students, between the ages of 18 and 30, with average French competency.

Participants must be in Paris for orientation in mid-September. Deadline for application is August 1.

Norway: Farm Work

Farms in Norway generally are very small and usually family-run. Participants live with a host family and take part in the daily life on the farm. Work involves performing various farm duties within a typical 35-hour work week. The length of stay ranges from a minimum of one month to a maximum of three months.

Free room and board are provided, plus weekly pocket money. The program fee is $225.

Requirements

There is no language requirement, but applicants must be between the ages of 18 and 30. Prior work experience is not necessary.

The deadline for applying is at least four months prior to the preferred starting date, no later than April 15.

Switzerland: Resort Work

Summer resort jobs are generally housekeeping, kitchen or dining-room positions that require hard work. The length of stay is two to three months during the summer high season, between July 1 and the end of September.

Most employers provide room and board. The program fee is $95.

Requirements

You must be a full-time student, between the ages of 18 and 30, and speak average to fluent German or French.

The deadline for applying is March 1.

Switzerland: Farm Work

Farming jobs in Switzerland are available to those who have a professional education or at least three years' practical experience in agriculture or horticulture. Placements are for two to four months between May and October.

The program fee is $95.

Requirements

You must speak average to fluent German or French and be between the ages of 18 and 30.

Au Pair Program

The purpose of the au pair program is to enable participants to learn about another culture by becoming integrated into a foreign society for an extended period of time. These positions require a great deal of adaptability, as the au pair lives with the host family, taking part in the daily activities and helping with household duties. Although the placement should not be considered a job, there is a great amount of responsibility involved in caring for children. Participants with outgoing personalities and a sense of independence do well. Placements are made in Austria, Germany, France, Denmark and Italy.

Applicants should apply at least three months prior to the desired starting date. Most families want the au pair to start in August or September. Summer placements also are available in France and Italy. InterExchange prearranges all placements. One placement is offered to each accepted applicant. InterChange does not guarantee that positions will be provided for all accepted applicants, in which case a refund, less a $10 administrative fee, will be made. Full refunds will be made for applications rejected by InterExchange. No refund will be made should the participant withdraw from the program at any time.

Program fees are $100 or $200, depending on the country.

Participants are responsible for paying travel expenses to and from the host country. Additionally, participants must be covered by health and accident insurance for the length of involvement in the program.

Room, board and monthly pocket money are provided. InterChange warns that this is not enough money to save for traveling.

Requirements

Au pair positions are available for females (males with the proper experience and references occasionally can be placed in Austria or Germany) between the ages of 18 and 25 (in France the age limit is 30) and require a commitment of six to 12 months. A commitment of one full year is preferred as this provides the family with continuity in child care and allows the participant enough time to understand and appreciate fully the culture.

For Austria, German language or agreement to take German classes in Austria is required; for France, two years of college-level French is required; for Germany, average German is required; and for Italy, some Italian is recommended.

Application Procedures for All Programs

Write to InterExchange to request a country kit or kits. Indicate if you are interested in a work-study program or the au pair program, and indicate the country(ies) in which you are interested. There is a $2.00 fee for each country kit requested. Each country kit includes an application, a country program description with salary and housing information, visa and work permit information, and insurance information.

Please note the application deadlines mentioned under each program.

Contact for All Programs:

InterChange, Inc.
356 West 34 Street
New York, NY 10001
telephone (212) 947-9533

Western Washington University in Bellingham, Washington, started a China Teaching Program (CTSP) in 1986. The program trains and places people to teach English as a second language for one year in the People's Republic of China.

Training sessions are for nine weeks in the fall, or an intensive six-week session in the summer. The training program includes teaching English as a foreign language, elementary Chinese, Chinese history and culture. Participants also are prepared for living and working in China. Placement is either as foreign teachers (those with a bachelor's degree) or foreign experts (those with a master's degree). Placements occur in September and February with various colleges, universities and institutions throughout China.

Participants receive a salary based upon their degree and experience. The host institution provides for internal travel, housing and medical care. Teachers must pay their own travel expenses to China, but most institutions pay the round-trip travel expenses of foreign experts. Tuition for the program is about $700 for Washington state residents and about $750 for others. Additional expenses for the training session are for housing, food, and approximately $100 for books and supplies.

Requirements

Applicants need to have at least an undergraduate degree and a desire to teach English as a second language. They must be flexible, motivated and willing to commit to a full year of teaching.

Application Procedures

Applications are due eight weeks before the start of each training session. CTSP can supply the exact dates, but the fall session generally starts in October, and the summer session in late June.

Contact:

China Teaching Program
Western Washington University
Erica Littlewood Work, Director
Old Main 530A
Bellingham, WA 98225-9047
telephone (206)676-3753

For more information on overseas jobs for U.S. citizens, explore these special resources available through Worldwise Books.

International Employment Hotline, edited by Will Cantrell. This monthly newsletter has been published since 1980. Each issue provides insider tips for job-hunters and announces new job vacancies in the government, private and non-profit sectors under country of assignment with job title, job description and employer contact. (12 issues/$36)

How to Find an Overseas Job with the U.S. Government, by Will Cantrell and Francine Modderno. This is a comprehensive guide to finding work with the organization that hires the greatest number of Americans to work abroad. The book has seventy chapters that include in-depth job descriptions and application procedures for 17 individual government agencies, with information on how to complete the government's application for employment (SF-171), and how to prepare for and pass the Foreign Service exam. ($28.95 postpaid)

The ISS Directory of Overseas Schools, by International Schools Services. Facilities and curricula for approximately 500 overseas schools are profiled in this directory. Information includes complete contact information for hiring authority. An excellent resource for teachers seeking overseas employment. ($30 plus $3 for shipping)

The International Consultant, by H. Peter Guttman. This book is a complete orientation for the aspiring consultant, covering such topics as: pursuing foreign prospects; writing proposals; negotiating a contract overseas; financing; joint ventures, foreign partners and representation; international arbitration; and more. ($22.95 plus $2 shipping)

Financial Resources for International Study, by the Institute of International Education. This is the first comprehensive listing of financial awards for U.S. citizens, both students and professionals, who want to study or work overseas. Each entry includes: sponsoring organization; amount and type of award; duration; eligibility; and application deadlines and procedures. ($36.95 plus $2 shipping)

To receive your personal copy of any of the above resources, send your order and payment to:

WORLDWISE™
B·O·O·K·S

Post Office Box 3030
Oakton, VA 22124